PIONEERS OF MODERN JAPANESE POETRY

PIONEERS OF MODERN JAPANESE POETRY

MURŌ SAISEI
KANEKO MITSUHARU
MIYOSHI TATSUJI
NAGASE KIYOKO

*Edited and Translated
with an Introduction by*

Takako Lento

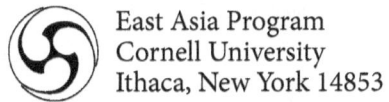

East Asia Program
Cornell University
Ithaca, New York 14853

The Cornell East Asia Series is published by the Cornell University East Asia Program (distinct from Cornell University Press). We publish books on a variety of scholarly topics relating to East Asia as a service to the academic community and the general public. Address submission inquiries to CEAS Editorial Board, East Asia Program, Cornell University, 140 Uris Hall, Ithaca, New York 14853-7601.

This volume is published with generous support by the Tanikawa Shuntarō Fund for publication of modern Japanese poetry.

Number 199 in the Cornell East Asia Series
Copyright ©2019 Takako Lento for English translations and text.
Original poetry copyright as follows:
Murō Saisei poetry ©2019 Murō Asako
Kaneko Mitsuharu poetry ©2019 Mori Touko
Miyoshi Tatsuji poetry ©2019 Miyoshi Kazuko
Nagase Kiyoko poetry ©2019 Inoue Nao
All rights reserved.

ISSN: 1050-2955
ISBN: 978-1-939161-09-3 hardcover
ISBN: 978-1939161-99-4 paperback
ISBN: 978-1942242-99-4 e-book
Library of Congress Control Number: 2018966303

Cover images:
Artist: Pogaryts'kyy. Stork in Japanese figures; shutterstock ID 152057054.
Artist: Umiberry. Traditional Japanese wave pattern; shutterstock ID702633058.
Cover design: Mai

CAUTION: Except for brief quotations in a review, no part of this book may be reproduced or utilized in any form without permission in writing from the author. Please address all inquiries to Takako U. Lento in care of the East Asia Program, Cornell University, 140 Uris Hall, Ithaca, NY 14853-7601.

CONTENTS

Personal Names xii
About This Book xiii
Acknowledgments xv

PIONEERS OF MODERN JAPANESE POETRY

INTRODUCTION:
PIONEERS IN THE DEVELOPMENT OF MODERN JAPANESE POETRY 3

Beginnings: "New Style Poetry" 6
Modern Japanese Poetry as Free Verse in the Vernacular 10
The Twenties: Energy and Frustration 11
The Thirties and Early Forties:
Repression, Censorship, and War 21
Postwar: Age of Democracy and Freedom of Speech 27
Four Poets after the War 31
Postwar Poets 34

MURŌ SAISEI 37
室生犀星 (1889–1962)
LIFE AND CAREER 39
POETRY 43

はる	46	47	Spring
朝の歌	48	49	Morning Song
故郷にて冬を送る	50	51	Winter in My Hometown
ドストエフスキイの肖像	52	53	A Portrait of Dostoyevsky
抒情小曲集 序曲	54	55	Lyrical Songs: Prelude
犀川	56	57	The River Sai
寂しき春	58	59	Lonely Spring
砂丘の上	60	61	On a Sand Dune
小さい家庭	62	63	A Small Home
音楽会の後	64	65	After a Concert
みな休息して	66	67	All in Repose
曙光を目ざして	68	69	Aiming at the First Light of Dawn
燃える	70	71	Aflame
夜半	72	73	In the Dead of Night
靴下	74	75	The Socks
我が家の花	76	77	The Flower of My Family
春の寺	78	79	The Temple in Spring
山なみ	80	81	Mountains
雪くる前	82	83	Before the Snow
己の中に見ゆ	84	85	What I See Inside Myself
駿河台の谷間	86	87	A Valley at Surugadai
み寺	88	89	The Temple
帰去来	90	91	I Will Leave
この人をみよ	92	93	Look at This Man
花	94	95	Flowers
鰯	96	97	The Sardine

三年山中	100	101	Three Years in the Mountains
昨日いらつしつてください	102	103	Please Come Back Yesterday
誰かに	104	105	Someone
老いたるえびのうた	106	107	Song of an Old Prawn

KANEKO MITSUHARU   109
金子光晴 (1895–1975)
LIFE AND CAREER   111
POETRY   117

金亀子	120	121	Gold Beetle
海の小品	122	123	Short Pieces on the Sea
古靴店	124	125	Used Shoe Shop
上水にて	126	127	On the Reservoir
寒山寺	128	129	Kanzanji Temple
ペダンの夜	130	131	Night in Pedang
燈台	132	133	The Lighthouse
洗面器	138	139	Washbasin
あけがたの歌 序詩	140	141	Song of Dawn: A Prefatory Poem
天使	144	145	Angels
卵の唄	148	149	A Song of the Egg
鬼と詩人	152	153	Ogres and Poet
昇天	154	155	Ascension
蛾 II	156	157	Moths II
蛾 III	158	159	Moths III
球	160	161	Globe
雨	164	165	Rain
富士	168	169	Mount Fuji

雪	172	173	Snow
霧	176	177	Fog
自叙伝について	180	181	On Autobiography
心	182	183	Heart
葦	184	185	Reeds

❖

MIYOSHI TATSUJI 193
三好達治 (1900–1964)
LIFE AND CAREER 195
POETRY 200

少年	204	205	The Youth
湖水	206	207	The Lake
村	208	209	A Village
鴉	210	211	Crow
信號	214	215	Signal
土	216	217	Earth
仔羊	218	219	Lamb
皿の中の風景	220	221	Scenery on a Plate
山鳩	222	223	Turtledove
自畫像	224	225	Self-Portrait
涙	228	229	Tears
あられふりける 二	230	231	Hail Comes Fluttering 2
桐の花	232	233	Paulownia Flowers
家庭	234	235	Family
毀れた窓	236	237	Broken Window
謎の音樂	240	241	Mysterious Music
ことのねたつな	242	243	May the Koto's Resonance Soar
わが名をよびて	244	245	Call My Name

我ら戦争に敗れたあとに	246	247	After We Were Defeated at War
胡桃讃	250	251	In Praise of the Walnut
村酒雑詠	252	253	Verses on a Village Brew
日もくれぬ	252	253	The Day Has Ended
盞は	252	253	The Saké-cup
死後の名は	252	253	A Posthumous Name
なつかしい斜面	254	255	This Slope Brings Back Memories
けれども情緒は	258	259	Yet, a Stirring in Me Seems
空のなぎさ	262	263	The Shore of the Sky

NAGASE KIYOKO 265
永瀬清子 (1906–1995)
Life and Career 267
Poetry 271

グレンデルの母親は	274	275	Grendel's Mother
諸国の天女	276	277	Heavenly Maidens on Earth
大いなる樹木	278	279	A Great Big Tree
早春	282	283	Early Spring
そよ風のふく日に	284	285	On a Day with a Gentle Breeze
踊りの輪	288	289	The Ring of Dancers
夜に燈ともし	290	291	Burning a Light at Night
美しい国	292	293	Beautiful Country
だましてください言葉やさしく	294	295	Humor Me with Your Sweet Words

女のうたえる	296	297	Song of a Woman
木陰の人	298	299	You in the Shade of a Tree
なぜこんなに	302	303	Why Like This
焰について	304	305	Flames
渦	306	307	Vortex
束の間	308	309	The Fleeting Moment
苗	310	311	Seedlings
夜あけ	312	313	Dawn
私の足に	314	315	To Fit My Feet
蛇	316	317	Snake
私は地球	318	319	I Am the Earth
第三の眼	322	323	A Third Eye
石炭と思って	326	327	Believing It Was Coal
ライバルは「死」であった	328	329	My Rival Was Death
あけがたにくる人よ	330	331	To You Who Come at Dawn
老いたるわが鬼女	334	335	My Aged Demon
黙っている人よ 藍色の靄よ	338	339	My Dear Silent One, My Indigo Mist
短章	342	343	Aphorisms
トラックが来て私を轢いたとき	342	343	When a Truck Comes and Runs Over Me
詩人とは何か	342	343	What Is a Poet?
詩を書く理由	342	343	Why I Write Poetry
詩は	344	345	Poetry Is
詩にリズムが	344	345	Poetry Needs Rhythm

A Note on Translation   347

Chronology of Poets' Lives   351
   Murō Saisei   353
   Kaneko Mitsuharu   357
   Miyoshi Tatsuji   362
   Nagase Kiyoko   366

Sources   371
   Murō Saisei   371
   Kaneko Mitsuharu   374
   Miyoshi Tatsuji   376
   Nagase Kiyoko   378

Bibliography   381

PERSONAL NAMES

This book follows Japanese convention with respect to personal names. Full Japanese names are given as family name (surname) first, given name last.

ABOUT THIS BOOK

Pioneers of Modern Japanese Poetry presents four distinguished modern Japanese poets: Murō Saisei, Kaneko Mitsuharu, Miyoshi Tatsuji, and Nagase Kiyoko. They lived and wrote through most of the twentieth century, a turbulent time in the history of Japan that encompassed the culturally open-minded and energized decade of the 1920s, the subsequent period of military fascism and the Pacific war, and the post–World War II democratic era. Together they produced an impressive body of work that demonstrates the breadth and depth of modern Japanese poetry.

Their poetry forms the main body of the book. Each poet is represented by a substantial selection of his or her work, presented in the original Japanese with an English translation on facing pages. A brief discussion of the poet's life, career, and poetry prefaces the selection. A general Introduction shows the four poets' achievements and contributions in the context of the evolution of modern Japanese poetry in the twentieth century.

The Sources section at the end of the book includes publication information on the Japanese text translated here. All translations of poetry and critical or historical quotes are by the author.

ACKNOWLEDGMENTS

First and foremost I would like to express my gratitude to the copyright holders for Murō Saisei, Kaneko Mitsuharu, Miyoshi Tatsuji, and Nagase Kiyoko. They generously granted permission for the use of the poets' work in the original Japanese and in my English translations, making it possible to assemble a substantial selection of these major modern poets.

I also wish to thank Mr. Tanikawa Shuntarō for advising me on the selection of the poets. I have long admired them, and was thrilled to translate their work. As I set out to do the translations, organize the book, and research the introduction, I came to further appreciate Mr. Tanikawa's deep insight into modern Japanese poetry. I am grateful for his guidance, encouragement, and patience in the course of this project.

I must note that this book was created in part because of Mr. Tanikawa's vision of making modern Japanese poetry available worldwide. As a means to realize his vision, he established the permanent Tanikawa Shuntarō Fund at Cornell University specifically to help the Cornell East Asia Series (CEAS) publish modern Japanese poetry and literary criticism in English translation.

The idea of presenting modern Japanese poets in a bilingual edition was brewed some years ago over a cup of tea with Mai Shaikhanuar-Cota, Managing Editor of CEAS. Our purpose in having the Japanese original and English translation side by side is to make the book more satisfying for readers who understand both languages, and more useful to those who are learning Japanese or studying Japanese poetry. Even to those who read this book simply to enjoy modern Japanese poetry in English, the presence of the Japanese original may be of interest. I am grateful for Mai's editorial acumen and unfailing support in seeing this project through.

Finally I thank my husband, Thomas V. Lento, Ph.D. He has been my first reader, literary critic and advisor, and cultural and linguistic consultant. I deeply appreciate his unfailing support and encouragement while I was completing this project.

PIONEERS OF MODERN JAPANESE POETRY

INTRODUCTION

Pioneers in the Development of Modern Japanese Poetry

Murō Saisei (1889–1962), Kaneko Mitsuharu (1895–1975), Miyoshi Tatsuji (1900–1964), and Nagase Kiyoko (1906–1995) are major figures in the development of modern Japanese poetry. They were among the pioneering generation of poets who, in the early decades of the twentieth century, broke with tradition to write free verse using vernacular language. They continued to produce distinguished work through the turmoil of World War II and into the postwar years.

Murō's intensely lyrical free verse was the first of its kind to be widely acclaimed and popularly admired. He led the lyrical poetry movement, and helped nurture the next generation by supporting younger poets and hosting gatherings for them at his home. Kaneko, on the other hand, was a loner and a rebel. He established a style unlike anyone else's, intentionally fusing what he learned from studying European contemporary poets during his sojourn in Brussels and Paris in the early 1920s with elements of the Japanese literary tradition. Miyoshi, an ardent admirer of Murō, came of age as a modernist poet in the late 1920s. By extending Murō's lyrical poetry movement he led the evolution of his fellow poets into modernist lyricists. Finally, Nagase, a resolute feminist in an era when women were expected to be subservient to men, was determined to be a poet from the time she was eighteen. Her faith in the power of womanhood and motherhood was evident and consistent throughout her work. Her poetry was intensely focused and stylistically ahead of her time, which later in her life earned her recognition by her peers as a pioneer of modern Japanese poetry.

The contributions of these four poets to the foundational development of modern Japanese poetry are significant, and their stature is undeniable. Today, all four poets are recognized as masters in the canon of modern Japanese poetry. Taken as a whole, their work serves as a landmark in mapping the varied and broad terrain of twentieth-century modern Japanese poetry. The poetry retains its freshness and power to this day, and continues to touch the hearts of twenty-first century readers.

The four poets came from different backgrounds and took different paths to artistic maturity and recognition. Murō Saisei's first book of lyrical poetry was received with enthusiasm by poets, novelists, and the reading public alike, and triggered the lyrical poetry movement in modern Japanese poetry. Many writers who admired his poetry gathered in his study, propelling him to the center of the movement. He in turn supported their poetic endeavors. Miyoshi Tatsuji was one of Murō's young admirers, and went on to sustain and further develop lyrical poetry as a major current in modern Japanese poetry. But while Murō and Miyoshi are both seminal figures in the evolution of modern lyrical poetry, they are distinctively different in their interests, temperaments, and poetic concerns.

By contrast, Kaneko Mitsuharu and Nagase Kiyoko stood outside of the major currents of their times, quietly forging substantial bodies of work in the face of serious personal and political constraints. They were not popular or powerful literary figures during their early careers, though they did have a number of peers and readers who recognized their rare talent. Their work was finally widely recognized and fully appreciated when the democratic world of postwar Japan held out the promise of free speech and gender equality.

What Murō, Kaneko, Miyoshi, and Nagase do have in common is that all were born into an era of radical social and cultural upheaval. The Imperial Constitution, which defined the structure and institutions of Imperial Japan as a constitutional monarchy designed to vie with the world powers of the day, was promulgated in the year Murō was born. That was two decades after the Meiji Restoration[1] of 1868. In that short period of time Japan had transformed itself from an isolated agrarian feudal society into a modern industrial nation-state. Seventeen years later, when Nagase, the youngest poet of the four, was born in 1906, Japan had already assumed its place as a military power by defeating czarist Russia in the Russo-Japanese war of 1904–1905.

This period of rapid sociopolitical development produced profound cultural dislocations among the Japanese people, but it was also an exciting time for discovering new ideas and systems of thought. In the literary arena the charged air of a society suddenly open to ideas from abroad, aided by the increasing availability of printing technology, spurred the development of publishing and mass media in the late nineteenth century, from opinion journals to popular magazines and daily newspapers.[2] Part of the mass media's self-appointed mission was to enlighten the masses. They found a ready audience for foreign literature, including contemporary novels and poetry. It was not only the mass media that thrived; specialized publications were welcomed by an eager readership as well.

These were promising times for literary entrepreneurs who wanted to test novel ideas in the intellectual marketplace. Such was the environment in which three young educators published *Shintaishi shō*

---

1. In 1868 the young Meiji Emperor officially restored the direct governing power of the Japanese throne, reasserted his divine lineage, and set out to create a modern nation. The process of implementation of the Emperor's progressively revolutionary vision of a modern nation state is presented in great detail in Chapter 16 of *Emperor of Japan* by Donald Keene (Columbia University Press, 2002), and Chapters 11 through 14 of *The Making of Modern Japan* by Marius B. Jansen (Harvard University Press, 2002).

2. Examples of the development of mass media in the late nineteenth century include the establishment of both *Yomiuri shinbun* (The Yomiuri newspaper), a daily newspaper, and *Meiroku zasshi* (Meiroku magazine) in 1874. Both were edited to appeal to and enlighten common people. *Jogaku zasshi* (Women's study magazine), focused on improving women's status, rights, and happiness, was founded in 1885. *Kokumin no tomo* (The nation's friend), its title taken from the U.S. weekly *The Nation*, was first published in 1887. This magazine, whose stated principles were liberalism, egalitarianism, and pacifism, published translations of masterworks of American, British, European and Russian fiction and poetry.

(Selection of New Style poetry), and saw their approach open the path for modern Japanese poetry to develop and thrive.

BEGINNINGS
"New Style Poetry"

Itō Sei[3] gives a vivid account of how *Shintaishi shō* came about.

In a corner of the Tokyo Imperial University campus was the publication department of the Ministry of Education, which compiled and edited textbooks, translations, and the like, issued by the Ministry. In 1882 Inoue Tetsujirō, who was twenty-eight years old, was working there to compile a history of Oriental philosophy. ... One day in March Yatabe Ryōkichi, a thirty-one-year-old botanist, came to ask for his advice. He had translated several lines from *Hamlet* starting with "To be or not to be" into a seven- and five-syllable pattern. In those days, Japanese poetry generally consisted of *tanka* and haiku. In addition to these, there was a form called *chōka* (long-poem) that also repeated the seven-five syllable pattern. This form had existed since *Man'yō shū*,[4] but had not been in general use for a long time. Longer poems were generally written in Chinese instead. To use a repetition of seven-five syllables to translate foreign poetry or to write original poetry was a novel attempt at the time.

Inoue Tetsujirō, [also] an expert writer of poetry in Chinese, said the attempted translation was interesting. Encouraged by Inoue, Yatabe not only translated but also wrote original poems using this form. Eventually Yatabe's colleague, Sotoyama Shōichi, a psychology professor, translated some poetry in seven-five syllable patterns and asked for Inoue's advice. Drawn by their attempts, Inoue himself composed his own poetry in this new style.

---

3. Itō Sei (1905–1969) was a prolific author of poetry, novels, literary criticism, literary history, and literary translations, as well as an educator. His work is collected in the 24-volume *Itō Sei zenshū* (Complete works of Itō Sei) (Shinchōsha, 1972–1974).

4. *Man'yō shū* (Collection of ten thousand leaves) is Japan's oldest existing collection of poetry. The collection, in twenty volumes, contains approximately 4,500 poems composed by people from all walks of life, ranging from emperors to common people, covering approximately 350 years prior to 759, when it was assembled.

Toyama Masakazu was one of the students who had been sent to London for study under the auspices of the Tokugawa Shōgunate. The textbooks he used there included poetry by Shakespeare, [Charles] Kingsley, [Thomas] Campbell, Tennyson, and others. He translated some poems by these poets, and also attempted to write his own. The three men compiled their translations and original poems and published a collection of poetry titled *Shintaishi shō* (Selection of New Style poetry) in July of that year through Maruzen, which was the importer and publisher of notable books at the time.

Shintaishi shō was immediately useful in providing lyrics for European-style songs to be taught in elementary and secondary schools, which helped [New Style poetry] to circulate widely. In terms of poetic technique the poems were roughhewn, but easier to understand compared to poetry in Chinese, and were not meaninglessly stylized like *tanka* or haiku, so young people happily welcomed them, singing those put to music, or reciting those that were not.[5]

Inoue Tetsujirō's note in *Shintaishi shō* amounts to a manifesto for this new form of poetry: "The songs of the Meiji Era must be songs of our era, not songs of the past. Japanese poetry must be in the Japanese language, not in Chinese. This is why we write poems in the new style."[6]

Shintaishi shō was a revolutionary event in that it marked the first conscious attempt to devise a new modern form of Japanese poetry. In its preface the authors explained why their new form of poetry was necessary to a modernizing Japan. First, a new long form was needed to express complex and cohesive ideas, which was not possible with the short *tanka* or haiku forms. Second, vernacular language was better suited to expressing contemporary thoughts and ideas. Last, a rhythmic pattern similar to the *chōka* (long verse) that appeared in *Man'yō shū* in effect provided a new mode of expression. In other words the authors proposed a verse form that could address the reali-

---

5. Itō Sei, "Early Modern Poets," in *Gendaishi no kanshō* I (Appreciating modern Japanese poetry vol. 1) (Tokyo: Meijishoin, 1968), 213–214.

6. *Shintaishi shō* was originally published by Maruya Zenshichi in 1882; it was reprinted by Kindai Bungakukan in 1971. The quote is from page 9/21, *Aozora bunko* Web-edition of the 1971 reprint.

ties of modern life by melding contemporary diction and unlimited lines with the traditional seven-five syllable poetic cadence.

As Yoshida Seiichi[7] observes, their concept quickly took root, but it was still tied to a traditional cadence. Yoshida gives New Style poetry its due while pointing out its limitations:

> Thus the New Style poetry was born. However, as they themselves called it "new style similar to *chōka*" it did not go beyond the confines of archaic *chōka* [in style and rhythm] with a five-seven or seven-five-based cadence. And even though it was indeed new and fresh, since they used diction very close to vernacular, and presented [new] thoughts and ideas (although many of them were imports), they were not equipped to pursue the matter of rhythm or cadence further, as they were not conversant with forms of poetry, being neither literary writers nor poets.
>
> Even though it was immature as poetry, their New Style poetry met the demands of the time ...[8]

Quality of poetic achievement aside, New Style poetry captured the imagination of poets, publishers, and readers to the extent that the term *"shintaishi"* (New Style poetry) appeared in a significant number of titles of poetry books in the decade following the publication of *Shintaishi shō*, and grew to be the dominant subject of discourse about poetic form and theory. It even appeared as a category in *Bunko* (Library),[9] a submission-based magazine directed to students at the

---

7. Yoshida Seiichi (1908–1984) was a literary critic and scholar of Japanese literature. His teaching career included professorships at the University of Tokyo and the Tokyo University of Education and a visiting professorship at the University of Michigan. His publications, including over thirty books, cover the history of Japanese literature, the history of literary criticism and literary theory, and studies of individual novelists and poets and of modern poetry in general.

8. Yoshida, "Kindaishi no nagare—kōgo jiyūshi no kakuritsu" (Development of early modern poetry—establishment of free verse in spoken language), in Itō Sei, Yoshida Seiichi, Bundō Junsaku, Koumi Eiji, eds., *Gendaishi no kanshō 2* (Appreciating modern Japanese poetry vol. 2) (Tokyo: Meijishoin, 1968), 8.

9. *Bunko* (Library) was a monthly submission-based magazine targeted for middle-school level students. It published 246 issues from 1895 until its termination in 1910.

middle-school level, with contents sourced from readers. One of *Bunko*'s five sections was dedicated to "*shintaishi*, *tanka*, haiku, and poetry in Chinese." This indicates a clear recognition of *shintaishi* as an established poetic genre, on equal footing with older forms.

It should be noted that *Bunko*'s editorial policy of accepting submissions from the public, and selecting contents based on peer review, set the pattern for many later poetry magazines and coterie publications. In succeeding decades these publications also gave group members, contributors, and readers an open forum for sharing their aesthetics, poetics, experiments, and creative output. Some of the magazines built a sizeable stable of contributing writers and attracted a large number of enthusiastic readers, creating powerful centers of influence in the development of modern Japanese poetry. That is why discussions of modern Japanese poetry, including this introduction, all reference these magazines, their editors, the poets associated with them, and how they fared in the world of poetry.

New Style poetry thrived, establishing the foundation of a new genre of poetry that better reflected modern Japan. But its traditional seven-five poetic cadence tended to invite poets to favor subject matter and diction reminiscent of the aesthetics of the past. Even though these verses were masterfully written and popularly acclaimed, they were not yet totally free from traditional constraints. For this reason New Style poetry is classified in Japanese literary history today as *kindaishi*,[10] or early modern Japanese poetry, which is a subset of modern Japanese poetry.

---

10. *Kindaishi* is the term that refers to poetry written primarily in the Meiji period (1868–1912) and for several years that followed.

MODERN JAPANESE POETRY AS FREE VERSE IN THE VERNACULAR

Soon poets began to free themselves from the traditional seven-five cadence in order to capture an immediacy of experience or convey contemporary attitudes and ideas. They eventually came to adopt a form completely liberated from tradition, combining free verse with vernacular language in the manner of common speech. This is now called *gendaishi* (modern Japanese poetry).[11] It is "common knowledge [among literary critics]," according to Ōoka Makoto,[12] that *gendaishi* became the prevalent poetic form in the early 1920s, a few years prior to the Shōwa Era (1926-1989).[13]

Murō was among the early innovators who wrote free verse during the transitional period. Professor Yoshida credits Murō's first two books, collections of lyrical poems written in free verse, as marking the arrival of *gendaishi*.

> Above all, *Ai no shishū* (Poems of love) (January 1918) and *Daini ai no shishū* (Poems of love II) (May 1919) were significant influences on a wide range of people. … All the poems in *Ai no shishū* are in free verse and common speech, and his spirits are expressed in somewhat awk-

---

11. *Gendaishi*: Yoshida Seiichi considers it as free verse in spoken language. "Kindaishi no nagare II—Kōgo jiyūshi no kakuritsu" (Development of early modern poetry II—Establishment of free verse in spoken language), Itō et al., eds., *Gendaishi no kanshō 2* (Appreciating modern Japanese poetry vol. 2), 1–19.

12. Ōoka Makoto (1931-2017) was a prolific poet in both traditional and modern forms, as well as a literary critic, essayist, art critic, and educator. His critical writing on modern Japanese poetry reflects his multifaceted literary experiences as a highly acclaimed poet, theorist, and scholar: he was visiting professor at Oakland University, MI, in 1981; he offered five lectures at *Collège de France* in 1994–1995; he was the 1996 Golden Wreath laureate of Struga Poetry Evenings in Macedonia. During his long career he received many honors for his poetry, criticism, and literary achievements, including the Order of Cultural Merit from the Japanese government in 2003 and the National Order of the Legion of Honour (*Ordre national de la Légion d'honneur-officier*) from France in 2004.

13. Ōoka, Makoto. *Shōwa shishi* (History of poetry in Shōwa Era) (Tokyo: Shichōsha, 1977), 10.

ward sentences ... but their sensory beauty filled with his honest feelings outshines all others.[14]

Ai no shishū (Poems of love), Murō Saisei's first book of poetry, caused a sensation in Japan's literary circles, as well as with the general public. Later that same year he published *Jojō shōkyoku shū* (Lyrical songs), which included poems first published in the magazine *ZAMBOA*,[15] edited by Kitahara Hakushū.[16] Murō's poems in *ZAMBOA* connected Murō with Hagiwara Sakutarō,[17] who called Murō his mentor. The two remained partners in poetry for life. These books firmly established Murō Saisei as a leading lyrical poet. Prominent writers, both poets and novelists, visited Murō to pay respect and to express their admiration, and Murō mentored many younger poets and supported their causes over the coming years. Enthusiasm generated by his intense lyricism, expressed in his own unique and straightforward free verse, made Murō, along with Hagiwara, central to the lyrical movement in modern Japanese poetry.

THE TWENTIES
Energy and Frustration

Japan emerged as a fledgling world power in the Russo-Japanese war, then solidified that position in World War I (1914–1918). But its steady pursuit of political and military goals, backed by rapid indus-

---

14. Yoshida, "Kindaishi no nagare II—kōgo jiyūshi no kakuritsu" (Development of early modern Japanese poetry II—Establishment of free verse in spoken language) in *Gendaishi no kanshō* 2 (Appreciating modern Japanese poetry 2), 17–18.

15. *ZAMBOA* was a poetry magazine edited by Kitahara Hakushū. Nineteen issues were published from 1911 to 1913. The magazine bears ZAMBOA in uppercase roman letters on the cover. *Zamboa* is a Portuguese word meaning a type of citrus fruit, evoking exotic Mediterranean flavors.

16. Kitahara Hakushū (1885–1942) was an influential master poet of New Style poetry, known for his beautiful cadences and lyricism.

17. Hagiwara Sakutarō (1886–1942) was a lyrical poet and literary theorist. His work *Shi no genri (Principles of Poetry)* was published by Cornell East Asia Program (1998) in English translation by Chester C.I. Wang and Isamu P. Fukuchi.

trialization, produced some undesirable consequences in the social sphere. In the agricultural sector poverty grew among small farmers as farmland was converted to industrial use. The new class of industrial workers faced poor labor conditions in the factories. These conditions, compounded by post–World War I recessions, spawned dissatisfaction and social unrest among the general public, creating fertile ground for sociopolitical activism in promoting the broad ideals of social democracy. In response to this growing social consciousness literary people, including poets, found themselves being drawn into the political and ideological debates of the day. This in turn prompted the government to take an increasingly hard line against opposition movements and any group that promoted ideas inconvenient to its imperialist policies.

In the midst of this charged environment a group of populist poets, who fervently believed in bringing art to their fellow citizens, founded the magazine *Minshū* (The people)[18] in 1918. Its objective was to provide a forum for presenting insightful slices of the reality of common life in vernacular language with the rhythms of natural speech. Yoshida Seiichi writes:

> Populist poets can be credited with popularizing free verse in everyday language and thereby bringing poetry closer to the masses. In our country World War I was proclaimed as a battle for democracy by Allied Forces against German militarism, which in part contributed to a surge of democratic thought starting in the fourth and fifth year of our country's Taisho Era [1912–1926]. The populist poets touted democratic ideas even before prose writers such as novelists or essayists, and made democracy their poetic motif. Their activities reached a pinnacle around May of 1919 when the centennial of Whitman's birth was celebrated.

Shiratori Shōgo,[19] who was the most earnest promoter of populist poetry, lists the following as major characteristics of populist poetry ("Study of Modern Poetry"):

---

18. *Minshū* (The people) published sixteen issues between 1918 and 1921. Contents included poetry, tanka, novels, plays, and essays.

19. Shiratori Shōgo (1890–1973) was a populist poet, known for his translation of Walt Whitman's poetry.

1. Having a positive desire to leap into the future through a passionate connection with the current state of affairs
2. Steadfast realism, derived from a broad survey of materials, finding poetry in all human beings and all matters of life that the poets of the past did not come to realize
3. Use of words that is free and clear.[20]

Populist poetry proved popular with readers, and its focus on spoken language in natural rhythms played a significant role in the development of modern Japanese poetry. Yet as a whole its artistic achievements have not been given the recognition they deserve. This is at least in part because contemporary poets such as Kitahara Hakushū, a powerful voice and a firm believer in traditional literary aesthetics and cadences, strongly objected to the populists' principles and practices. His attitude is echoed in Professor Yoshida's statement that "the fatal issue associated with this populist poetry was that it was verbose, its use of words insensitive, and its imagination dull and prosaic."[21]

There can be no doubt, however, that populist poetry contributed greatly to the establishment of free verse as the form of *gendaishi*, or modern Japanese poetry, through its unyielding focus on using forthright natural speech. Populist poetry had a thematic impact as well. Its depiction of the realities of the everyday life of the common people touched its readers and became a continuing current in the world of poetry.

While lyrical poetry captured the imagination of the literary world and a large popular audience, and populist poetry was establishing realism as a strong current, other poets were being inspired by avant-garde movements imported from the West such as futurism, Dadaism, anarchism, and socialism. Given the social and economic stress of the period the urge to question and rebel against received values and existing constraints was strong, particularly among the younger

---

20. Yoshida, "*Kindaishi no nagare* II—*kōgo jiyūshi no kakuritsu*" (Development of early modern Japanese poetry II—Establishment of free verse in spoken words), "*Gendaishi no kanshō* 2" (Appreciating modern Japanese poetry 2), 16.

21. Ibid., 17.

generation. In 1920 Dadaism excited the imagination of nineteen-year-old Takahashi Shinkichi when he read a couple of local newspaper articles about it. Such was the thirst of the Japanese public for new ideas and information that a regional daily newspaper covered an avant-garde movement in France, and that a local youth would be so inspired by it that he became a leading figure of the avant-garde movement. Takahashi recalled that experience decades later:

> At the time I had no friends I could discuss this with, and all I could do was dream of the unknown distant city of Paris ... What moved me the most was the way the letters were arranged on the page—vertically, horizontally, and even diagonally.[22]

The following year Takahashi became a servant at a Buddhist temple of the esoteric Shingon sect, then moved to Tokyo and began to associate with poets. When he published *Dadaisuto Shinkichi no shi* (Poems of Dadaist Shinkichi) in 1923, his poems shocked and resonated with his young contemporaries. It should be noted, however, that his "Dadaism" was colored by what he absorbed from his brush with esoteric Buddhism, and thus diverged in some respects from the original Dadaism.

Takahashi Shinkichi's personalization of Dadaism is fairly typical of the way modern Japanese poets adapted foreign elements or ideas to incorporate into their creative work. Takahashi is called "Dadaist" in literary discussions in Japan because he was first inspired by Dadaism, even though his work is an admixture of a native Buddhist sensitivity with alien aesthetic concepts. This process of adapting foreign influences to the poet's own personal and cultural needs and sensibilities is hardly unique to Japan, of course. But the reader should keep in mind that even when a Japanese literary movement is named after a foreign influence, it may be quite different from its namesake in its purpose, poetics, or methodology.

Another modernist landmark, with a resolutely destructionist intent, also appeared in 1923: the first issue of *Aka to kuro* (Red and

---

22. Takahashi Shinkichi, "Dadaist Movement in Japan," *Poetics*, May 1963. Cited in Ōoka, *Shōwa shishi* (Poetry of Shōwa Era) (Tokyo: Shichōsha, 1977), 20.

black).²³ Its manifesto reads in part: "What is poetry? What is a poet? We abandon the entire past and boldly declare 'Poetry is a bomb! A poet is a dark lawbreaker who throws bombs at the sturdy walls and doors of the prison.'"²⁴ Tsuboi Shigeji,²⁵ its editor and publisher, later recalled those days:

> Back then populist poetry was going strong, and we were frustrated with their poetry, which we found lukewarm and mannered. We were not only frustrated with the populist poetry group, but we also wanted to negate all existing systems and concepts. We had a ferocious urge to apply a red-hot iron to all that was facing us.²⁶

Unfortunately their revolutionary resolve attracted the scrutiny of the increasingly oppressive authorities, who were intent on purging anti-government activities and views.

The same year saw Murō Saisei publish his eighth book of lyrical poetry, *Aoki uwo o tsuru hito* (The man fishing blue fish), as well as the second edition of *Jojō shōkyoku shū* (Lyrical songs), proof that lyrical poetry was still thriving. This was also the year Kaneko Mitsuharu, another of the four poets featured in this book, published his first book of poetry *Koganemushi* (Gold beetle), which was unlike any other in style, theme, and tone. Kaneko had recently returned from his first stay in Europe where he lived in a village on the outskirts of Brussels, Belgium, for a full year, then in Paris for an additional half year. While abroad he had devoted himself to reading European con-

---

23. *Aka to kuro* (Red and Black) was an anarchistic coterie magazine established by Tsuboi Shigeji and three other poets who declared the negation of all as the basis for existence. Four issues were published from 1923 to 1924, with many words blanked out by censorship.

24. Andō Motoo, Ōoka Makoto, Nakamura Minoru, eds., *Gendaishi daijiten* (Encyclopedia of modern poetry) (Tokyo: Sanseidō, 2008), 13.

25. Tsuboi Shigeji (1897–1975) was a lifelong left-wing activist and poet. During the prewar years he was arrested and jailed many times because of his "dangerous" thoughts and activism, but as proletarian literary movements dwindled, he declared his ideological conversion in 1934 to secure a release from jail. After the war he was a founding member of left-leaning New Japan Literary Conference and was named its Central Officer in 1945.

26. Ōoka, *Shōwa shishi*, 24.

temporary poets, including symbolists and Parnassians, and studying their methods. He was given opportunities to associate socially with artists and distinguished art collectors. Kaneko recalled his aspiration to write poetry in his own way, which he had developed toward the conclusion of his European residency:

> When I took a pause from my devotion to Europe, I began to look back with fresh eyes at my old home country from a distance. Japan appeared beautiful in my memories, joined with various emotions, but that might have been a mere shadow play created by nostalgia, which I did not think I had at the time. Even so, as I had formulated a method in my own way, I attempted with it to construct a palace of beauty no one had ever built before, although I had no idea if I was succeeding or not. Verhaeren's rhythms echoed aloof and hollow to me by then. Around the time I was to leave for Japan, my mind was preoccupied with the splendid and mystic, gilded and dazzling world of Gustave Moreau's decorative art and of Bengali miniature art. My youthful mind had come to be obsessed with the idea that my birthright mission was to seal the infinite kaleidoscope of life inside the shades of a single line of poetry. In short, I was a bit drunk with the intoxicating potion of the West.[27]

Even though Kaneko's recollection sounds characteristically sardonic, he was privately confident that *Koganemushi* (Gold beetle) reflected his resolve to create "a palace of beauty no one had ever built before" by melding what he absorbed through experiencing European poetry and art with what he had accumulated from classic Japanese aesthetics through the voracious reading of his earlier years. Upon publication of *Koganemushi,* his friends, young aspiring poets themselves, were very impressed with what he achieved in fusing Japanese and Western elements, and Kaneko was hopeful about the success of his book. But before the broader world of poetry had time to pay attention to it, the Great Tokyo Earthquake of September 1923 devastated the entire Tokyo area, disrupting every aspect of life in the region.

---

27. Kaneko Mitsuharu, *Shijin: Kaneko Mitshuaru jiden* (Poet: Autobiography of Kaneko Mitsuharu) (Tokyo: Kōdansha, 1994), 96.

New developments came swiftly on the heels of this disaster, in both the literary and political arenas. Leftist political movements gained force, and proletarian poetry increased in appeal for the general public. *Tanemakuhito* (The sowers),[28] generally credited to be the first magazine for Proletarian poetry, was forced to cease publication after the quake, but its former members regrouped to publish the magazine *Bungei sensen* (Literary battlefront) in 1924. This publication was instrumental in the formation of the Japan Proletarian Literary Arts League in 1925. In the same year, the Peace Preservation Law was enacted to suppress Communism, but it was soon turned into a tool for silencing a broad spectrum of socialists and suppressing democratic activities.

In 1926 the magazine *Roba* (Donkey)[29] was founded by poets in Murō Saisei's circle, including notable lyrical poets such as Hori Tatsuo[30] and leftist poets such as Nakano Shigeharu.[31] Nakano's proletarian poetry and his essays on poetics appeared in its inaugural issue, which hardline proletarian poets severely criticized for its lack of activist rhetoric. Nakano was also involved in organizing Nippon

---

28. *Tanemakuhito* (The sower) was a coterie magazine that published twenty-four issues from 1921 to 1923. It was a progressive opinion magazine centered on antiwar sentiments and humanism.

29. *Roba (Donkey)*, a monthly literary magazine, was founded in 1926 by disciples of Murō Saisei, who supported it financially. Its last issue appeared in 1928. *Roba* published various genres of literature including poetry, translated poetry, criticism, essays, short stories, and even haiku. Contributors included proletarian and Marxist poets, lyrical poets, and modernist poets influenced by contemporary French poetry.

30. Hori Tatsuo (1904–1953) was a lyrical poet and novelist. He was an avid reader of Hagiwara Sakutarō's poetry. He began to write lyrical poetry after meeting Murō Saisei in 1923. His poetry was sensitive, pensive, and elegantly stylish, admired by fellow lyrical poets, and adored by an enthusiastic readership. He was at the center of the lyrical poetry scene until illness caused his premature death.

31. Nakano Shigeharu (1902–1979) was a poet and leftist activist. While in high school, he admired Murō Saisei's lyrical poems, visited him, and formed a long relationship with Murō as his mentor. As a Tokyo University student he was in the study group on Marxist Arts. In 1926 he teamed with poets, including Hori Tatsuo, to found *Roba* to which he contributed his early Proletarian poetry. His Proletarian poetry grew increasingly combative when he joined the Communist Party, which caused him to be incarcerated under the Peace Preservation Law. Although he was forced to renounce his leftist beliefs, he resumed his Proletarian activities and writing after the war ended.

Artista Proleta Federacio (NAPF) in 1928, and edited its journal *Senki* (Battle flag), which provided a forum for the mainstream Marxist literary movement. Hardliners in the leftist movement countered by organizing the Japan Proletarian Cultural League, advocating the use of poetry as agitation and propaganda for the masses. These energetic factions were influenced by socialist and communist movements overseas. Proletarian poetry from various factions was strong enough to compete with art-oriented non-political poetry in the twenties for recognition and popular attention.

Concurrent with these proletarian literary activities, and equally energized and ambitious, a younger generation of poets was focusing on art rather than politics. These poets were directly influenced by contemporary European and American poetry and the Modernist ideas that were flooding into Japan at the time. Aspiring young poets with an urge to pursue the modernism of the West and to rebel against the established world of poetry started a poetry magazine with the specific intent of providing a central forum for new types of modern poetry. In September 1928 they published the first issue of *Shi to shiron* (Poetry and poetics).[32] In their effort to distinguish themselves from their elders in the established world of modern poetry, the founding members were clear about their resolve to create a poetics of their own, focused on constructing an ésprit nouveau (new poetic spirit) with a fresh type of poetry that they called "*poésie*." In a postscript to the inaugural issue, founding editor Haruyama Yukio[33] wrote:

> The major purpose in publishing *Shi to shiron* (Poetry and poetics) magazine is to demonstrate what we believe to be the right thing to do in our world of poetry. What a joy to have this opportunity here and now to present today's *poésie* properly, having broken away from the monopolistic grip of an old guard who have no poetics of their own ...

---

32. *Shi to shiron* (Poetry and poetics), a quarterly magazine, published 14 issues from 1928 to 1931. After the fourteenth issue it changed its name to *Bungaku* (Literature) and continued until 1933.

33. Haruyama Yukio (1902–1994) was a poet, critic, translator, and magazine editor who effectively organized both poetic and cultural movements. He started out as a symbolist and grew to be an urban modernist.

This is the world of poetry in which we eleven members take the lead.[34]

These innovative younger poets had previously been publishing their work in small coterie magazines in various locales. For them to claim center stage in the world of modern poetry was an auspicious start to a movement.

One of the eleven founding members was Miyoshi Tatsuji, the third poet featured in this book. He had just graduated from the Department of French Literature at Tokyo Imperial University. During high school he had discovered and immersed himself in lyrical poetry by Murō Saisei and Hagiwara Sakutarō, whom Miyoshi called his master. Miyoshi had associated with literary-minded fellow students at the university while studying nineteenth-century French poetry, particularly Verlaine and Mallarmé, and started publishing poetry in coterie magazines. As a founding member of *Poetry and poetics*, Miyoshi became a driving force for introducing contemporary French poetry and poetics through his translations and critical essays on the subject. The inaugural issue of *Shi to shiron* (Poetry and poetics) showcased Miyoshi's exceptional versatility, including three of his poems, his essay "On Paul Verlaine (1)," and his translation of the *esquisse* (sketch) "Grandmother" by the French poet François Copée. His voluminous output of translations of French poetry and prose was legendary among his friends.

Shi to shiron (Poetry and poetics) attracted a broad range of contributors, generated enthusiasm about new types of poetry among poets and readers, and became a propulsive force behind lyrical, modernist, and art-for-art's-sake poetry. As a testament to its recognition, broad appeal, and reach in just its first year, Nagase Kiyoko, the youngest of the four poets featured in this book, noted in the entry for 1928 in the chronicle of her life: "My first daughter was born. Membership in *Shi no ie* (House of poetry) grew to over thirty. *Shi to shiron* (Poetry and poetics) was an overwhelming presence in the world of poetry."[35]

---

34. Ōoka, *Shōwa shishi*, 66.

35. Nagase Kiyoko, *Nagase Kiyoko shishū* (Poems of Nagase Kiyoko) (Tokyo: Shichōsha, 1979), 133.

Nagase was a dedicated member of *Shi no ie* (House of poetry), a small coterie poetry magazine presided over by her lifelong mentor Satō Sōnosuke,[36] whom both Murō Saisei and Kaneko Mitsuharu considered a brilliantly talented poet.

In 1928 Nagase was twenty-two years old and had just had her first child. Four years earlier, at eighteen, she had dedicated herself to poetry, enrolled in the English department of Aichi Prefectural Women's High School, and sent her poems to Satō Sōnosuke. In 1927 she had married the young man her parents had chosen for her on condition that she be allowed to continue writing poetry. She was determined to be a poet, while living a conventional woman's life in the countryside of Japan. In 1930 she published her first book of poetry, *Gurenderu no hahaoya* (Grendel's mother) with her mentor Satō's "powerful postscript," as she wrote in the chronicle of her life. Her trust and belief in the power of womanhood and motherhood are evident throughout her career, expressed through distinctively straightforward, precise, and clean verse. She credited this style to her mentor's advice in her youth. Paradoxically, her sustained focus on the realities of life takes readers to a realm beyond the mundane, yielding insights into universal truth.

Also in 1930, Miyoshi Tatsuji published his first book of poems, *Sokuryōsen* (Surveyor ship). The lyrical poems in this collection reflect his admiration for the work of Murō Saisei and Hagiwara Sakutarō, but they remain very much his own. His poems are characterized by an innovative and ambitiously fresh style that fuses native lyricism with the stylistic and philosophical influences of Western modernism. *Sokuryōsen* was an immediate success, passionately received and recognized as transformational by fellow poets while attracting an enthusiastic general readership. His continued effort to create new types and forms of lyrical poetry influenced and guided his fellow poets through the next decade.

---

36. Satō Sōnosuke (1890–1942) was a poet and editor. He published seventeen books of poetry. In 1943 Murō Saisei edited *Satō Sōnosuke zenshū* (Complete poems of Satō Sōnosuke, 2 volumes).

THE THIRTIES AND EARLY FORTIES
Repression, Censorship, and War

The 1930s saw the steady advance of Japanese military aggression in Asia, accompanied by a harsh and open assault on freedom of speech in the name of the divine Emperor at home. During this period the activities and publications of the leftist, democratic, and avant garde groups of the previous decade were pushed to virtual extinction. In 1931 the Manchurian Incident triggered martial law in Japan, which lasted until Japan's defeat in World War II in 1945. But the defining moment in the military regime's march toward unchecked control over the country came on May 15, 1932, when young naval officers assassinated Inukai Tsuyoshi,[37] the last prewar civilian prime minister.

As Ōoka Makoto points out, 1932 was also a watershed year in the history of Japanese literature. The authorities arrested the thinkers, writers, and activists in leftist movements, giving them the choice of renouncing their beliefs or facing incarceration. Ōoka quotes Honda Shūgo's[38] firsthand observation of the state of the literary world in the early to mid-1930s:

> Under these circumstances, while one "big figure" after another of the Communist Party renounced his political beliefs, the Proletarian Authors League could not hold meetings; or if it did, few attended. The publication of their bulletin *Puroretaria bungaku* (Proletarian literature) became sporadic, and even when published it had only a few pages. On the other hand new literary magazines such as *Bungakukai* (Literary world), *Kōdō* (Actions), and *Bungei* (Literary arts) published

---

37. Inukai Tsuyoshi (1855–1932), a veteran politician and government official, became prime minister on December 13, 1931. He tried to rein in the military, and was assassinated on May 15, 1932, in a coup d'état led by eleven young navy officers.

38. Honda Shūgo (1908–2001) was a literary critic and scholar. In 1929, while a student at Tokyo University, Honda became interested in Marxism. In 1930 he participated in a demonstration to commemorate the Russian revolution and was arrested. After World War II ended, he was a founding member of *Kindai bungaku* (Early modern literature), which published 185 issues over eighteen years and eight months starting in 1946. The magazine focused on issues such as generational differences, the interaction of politics and literature, and the relationships between organizations and individuals.

their first issues one after another, which caused people to talk about a "renaissance" in literature. ... Literary circles breathed a sigh of relief, as they no longer faced pressure from the left, but almost immediately they had to helplessly face heavy pressure from the extreme right. To begin with, it was only the leftists who had backbones strong enough to attempt open resistance against the heavy pressure from the right that used "the state of emergency." It was certainly true that "the circumstances that forced proletarian literature to decline brought about the phenomenon of a literary renaissance" (Kubokawa Tsurujirō).[39] Yet these same circumstances also restrained the nature and scope of this renaissance.[40]

To Honda's account Ōoka adds:

The renaissance in literature Honda speaks of in this brief observation occurs at approximately the time of the initial issues of *Shiki* (Four seasons) and *Rekitei* (Journey). In the world of poetry, and in terms of their circumstances, objectively speaking, his description also applies to these magazines.[41]

In the midst of the relentless military oppression of free speech, *Shiki* was founded as a quarterly in 1933, and restarted as a monthly, also called *Shiki*, in 1934. Hori Tatsuo was the original editor, enlisting Maruyama Kaoru[42] and Miyoshi Tatsuji as coeditors when it switched to monthly publication. Eighty-one issues of the monthly edition ap-

---

39. Kubokawa Tsurujirō (1903–1974) was a literary critic and proletarian poet. He was the founding publisher and editor of the literary magazine *Roba* (Donkey) in 1926.

40. *Shōwa bungaku shi* (History of Shōwa literature) (Tokyo: Kadokawa bunko, 1956), cited in Ōoka, *Shōwa shishi*, 95–96.

41. Ōoka, *Shōwa shishi*, 96.

42. Maruyama Kaoru (1899–1974) was a poet, essayist, novelist, and educator. While a student at the third school of higher education (now Kyoto University), he met fellow student Miyoshi Tatsuji and other aspiring poets and began to write poetry himself. In 1926 he entered Tokyo Imperial University, majoring in Japanese literature, and became a member of the poetry magazines *Shin-shichō* (New current) and *Shii no ki* (Beech tree). He was actively involved with *Shi to shiron* (Poetry and poetics) and the second *Shiki*. He revived (the fourth) *Shiki* in 1967. It ceased publication in 1977 with a memorial issue for Maruyama.

peared before *Shiki* ceased publication in 1944. When critics speak of the role of *Shiki* in the development of Japanese poetry, they are referring to this second, monthly edition. (The magazine was also restarted three more times after the war.)

Shiki, with its open-minded editorial policy, provided a forum for a wide range of contributors, including prominent figures such as Murō Saisei and Hagiwara Sakutarō as well as younger poets. The magazine printed works by more than three hundred poets in all, building a broad-based and enthusiastic readership in the process. Due to the leadership of Miyoshi Tatsuji, however, it became best known as a powerhouse of lyrical poetry, led by Miyoshi's own innovative poetic creations. In the aftermath of World War II Maruyama Kaoru analyzed the reasons for its popularity:

> Above all it [*Shiki*] was a magazine of lyrical poetry and involved the notable lyrical poets of the time. Besides, those poets were, relatively speaking, cultured and measured, generating an urbane and intellectual atmosphere resonating with the native lyrical tradition, which attracted poetry lovers who were craving [such lyricism].[43]

On the other hand, Yoshimoto Takaaki,[44] a poet and thinker of the next generation who was still a student during the war, saw an element of escapism in their work.

> The fact is that they [those who published in *Shiki*] were poets of Nature. ... They, like the poets of medieval Japan, lodged the world of their poetic imagination in the relationship between Nature and their internal being. ... [T]hese poets successfully brought the traditional sensibilities nurtured over the centuries in Japanese culture to the

---

43. Ōoka, *Shōwa shishi*, 112–113.

44. Yoshimoto Takaaki (1924–2012) was a poet, thinker, literary critic, and essayist. At the end of the war, in order to resolve the disjunction between his devout belief in military propaganda before and during the war and his recognition of postwar realities, he conducted an intense study of the economic theories of Adam Smith and Karl Marx as well as of ancient and classic Japanese literature. He acquired unique insight into the nature of language and literature and developed his own worldview, reflected in his prolific writing on Japanese literature, society, and culture.

conscious level [of modern man] through dialogues primarily with matters in Nature.[45]

Although Maruyama and Yoshimoto approach the topic from different perspectives, both observe that the *Shiki* group's poetry draws on a deep-rooted native Japanese sensibility. This sensibility, infused with Buddhist and Shinto concepts, is characterized by profound empathy with the natural cycle of life and death, embodied in an appreciation of life's glory combined with an acute awareness of its transience. This perspective can encourage passive surrender to the flow of nature as an escape from miseries at hand, while harboring a resilient hope for regeneration. The *Shiki* group immersed itself in these sentiments to "forge an orderly poetic imagination that can contend with the current state of affairs,"[46] as Ōoka puts it. More generally, lyrical poetry that expresses an inherent trust in nature's quiet but powerful regenerative force helped poets and readers mitigate the pain of having to face the harsh realities of the dark times in which they were living.

Rekitei (Journey), the other contemporary poetry magazine referred to by Ōoka as part of his observation of "the renaissance in literature," published its initial issue in 1935 and ceased publication in 1943. From its very inception this magazine was highly inclusive. It provided a home and outlet for many types of poets, from more nationalistic groups to left-leaning writers. Itō Shinkichi, a poet associated with the proletarian movement and a member of NAPF, speaks of *Rekitei*'s characteristics:

> The congregation of individualistic poets who were not academic or sentimental and did not write like translations from foreign poetry had cultural significance. In this context, *Rekitei* was idiosyncratic and against the trends of the time.[47]

---

45. Ōoka, *Shōwa shishi*, 114–115.
46. Ibid., 115.
47. Itō Shinkichi, *Gyakuryū no naka no uta* (Songs against the tide); cited in Ōoka, *Shōwa shishi*, 128.

Itō Shinkichi's approval of poets "who were not academic or sentimental and did not write like translations from foreign poetry" might be a sly reference to the modernists and lyricists associated with *Shiki*, since his fellow leftist poets were *Rekitei* contributors. But together the two poetry magazines were invaluable forums for poets, and as such helped sustain modern Japanese poetry during trying times.

On the sociopolitical front the military regime was intent on brainwashing citizens to believe that Japan was under divine protection and would prevail in all wars. If independent thinkers had any doubt about the legitimacy of this claim, they were well advised not to be vocal about it. Protesting against militarism could lead to jail or even death. But even in this oppressive environment Kaneko Mitsuharu was determined to speak his own mind.

In 1928, unsuccessful in poetry and business, Kaneko had gone to Europe with his wife to escape from a destitute life. They travelled by way of Southeast Asian coast towns, and arrived in Paris in 1930, where they survived on subsistence living for two years. In 1931, while they were in Paris, the Sino-Japanese war began. Kaneko observed that Japan's military aggression was not well received by the Europeans. On their way home by way of Singapore, Malaya, and China, he witnessed China's anti-Japanese sentiments for himself. These experiences gave him a more balanced perspective on the world at large and insight into the truth behind the Imperialist propaganda that was sweeping Japan. When he settled back in Japan in 1932, he was appalled at his fellow citizens' apathy in the face of ultranationalistic propaganda. As a left-leaning writer (though not a leftist activist), Kaneko dodged censorship to publish poems that denounced the fundamental structure and Imperialist policies of Japan. In 1935 he published poems such as "The Lighthouse."[48] He recalls the morning of February 26, 1936, when a failed coup d'état by a military faction led to fascism under full military control of the government:

---

48. "The Lighthouse" was published in the progressive general magazine *Chūō Kōron* at the urging of its editor, who was impressed with Kaneko's antiwar poems.

On the snowy cold morning, Kunikida[49] came, his face white, shaking all over, saying, "A horrific thing has happened!" News reports said that all the cabinet members were killed in the military coup d'état ... I felt that it was somehow expected .... Back then we lived in a rental house with a small yard where an impressive boxwood tree stood. Kunikida had brought with him a bunch of leftist publications. I used a hoe to turn over the snow and dirt and dug a hole under the boxwood and buried all of the publications. I felt the danger hanging over my friend, and also over me.[50]

Yet in spite of this danger he had the courage to publish *Same* (Sharks), a collection of well-camouflaged antiwar and resistance poems, through Jinminsha (The Masses Press) in 1937.

In addition to systematically suppressing proletarian and leftist poets and their publications, the authorities used economic pretexts to force all other groups of poets to consolidate. According to a historical account from the Japan Poets Association there were four poets' associations in 1941 when the Pacific War started, but in 1942 they were ordered to merge into one national organization to support the government's nationalistic cause. In 1943 the approximately two hundred literary magazines then in existence were also consolidated into sixty-two publications. That number was reduced to two in 1944.[51] Even those two eventually disappeared because their publishing house burned down during the air raids over Tokyo.

Naturally many poets who did not support the war found this period agonizing. Some fell silent. Murō Saisei wrote mostly novels, colored with nostalgia for the ancient graces, which sold well. Kaneko Mitsuharu had no outlets, yet continued to write, in secret, poems defiantly opposing the authorities, their core ideology, and war in general. There were others, however, who wrote enthusiastically about the war effort and trumpeted Japan's inevitable victory. Miyo-

---

49. Kunikida Torao (1902–1970) was a poet known for his sensitive lyricism. He participated in a proletarian film movement, and was active as a movie script writer.

50. Kaneko, *Poet*, 184.

51. "History and Origin" section on Japan Poets Association's official website: www.japan-poets-association.com.

shi Tatsuji wrote three well-received volumes of poetry in praise of military conquest. The government used such poetry as a tool to glorify and boost support for the war. Established poets were practically forced to contribute appropriate pieces to a patriotic anthology of poetry, and many complied, willingly or unwillingly. Nagase Kiyoko submitted two poems to *Tsuji shishū* (Tsuji collection of poems) in response to a request from Nihon bungaku hōkokukai (Patriotic Association of Japanese Writers) in 1943, and saw them subjected to editorial rewrites and errors as she noted later. Meanwhile promising young poets were drafted into the military, many of whom died on the battlefield or due to wounds, malnutrition, or illness. Ironically this was the period of time when poetry had its greatest exposure to the broad Japanese public because of the daily broadcast of government-approved poetry as part of the nation's effort to fan patriotic fervor among its people.

POSTWAR
Age of Democracy and Freedom of Speech

In August 1945, in an extraordinary radio broadcast to his people, the Emperor of Japan announced that the war had ended in defeat. Under the terms of surrender he renounced all claims to divinity and political power. The Japanese people suddenly found themselves unburdened of the myth of divine protection and freed from military dictatorship and oppression, although under occupation by the Allied Forces. Total disbelief, disruption, and confusion ensued in the war-ravaged land, but it was short-lived, as the Allied occupation forces focused on maintaining order and establishing democracy.

Fortunately the ideal of democracy was not a foreign concept to the Japanese. They had been exposed to the concepts of freedom, equality, and democracy decades earlier through the various democratic movements that had existed prior to the imposition of military control. Thus when the postwar Constitution of Japan, written under strong Allied influence and promulgated in 1947, proclaimed the nation's resolve to uphold the principles of democracy and maintain peace with no standing military forces, the people were ready to accept it. When Japan regained its independence in 1952, with the Emperor redefined as a national symbol rather than a divine ruler, it embarked on a period of remarkable economic growth, rebuilding out of war-torn rubble with the same resilience, discipline, and energy that had transformed it from a feudal country into a modern nation just a few decades earlier.

Those qualities of resolve, perseverance, and commitment to rebirth prevailed among the country's poets and writers as well. Immediately after the announcement of defeat they began to examine the meaning of their lives, their experiences during the prewar and wartime periods, and the potential of the new age. Poets of all schools, old and young, regardless of their beliefs, were free to write in their own voices. Now they could "speak good thoughts with no scruples," as Nagase Kiyoko joyfully wrote.[52]

Kihara Kōichi[53] recollects how his fellow poets survived the war and how quickly they responded to the radical changes in his "Story of Post–World War II Poetry":

> When the war ended not a single poetry magazine was being published in Japan. In 1944, all the poetry magazines in Japan had been consolidated into two publications, *Nihon shi* (Japanese poetry) and *Shi kenkyū* (The study of poetry). The first issue of *The Study of Poetry* was June 27, 1944. I received it the day before I was to leave for Iwō Jima. I don't know how many issues were published after that. But it is a fact that for several months after the air raids on Tokyo started, neither *Japanese Poetry* nor *The Study of Poetry* were published. Their printing house and the publisher, Hōbunkan, had vanished in the air raid fires.
>
> Back then the only way left for poets to have their poetry read was to exchange poems by mail. In Tokyo, Kitazono Katsue and others

---

52. "Beautiful Country," Nagase Kiyoko, *Utsukushii kuni* (Beautiful country) (Tokyo: Irorishobō, 1948).

53. Kihara Kōichi (1922–1979) was known as a promising young avant-garde poet before the war, and was a prominent member of the *Arechi* group during the postwar era.

formed *Mugi tsūshin* (Wheat correspondence), while Okada Yoshihiko and others had *Tsūshin* (Correspondence) in Kyūshu. There were some other groups as well, and poets were reading each other's work in secret. It was what you might call a supply line for minds in the middle of war. Many poets were drafted to be soldiers; some were stranded in foreign lands. Kuroda Saburō was in Java, Ayukawa Nobuo and Nakagiri Masao were hospitalized in Army hospitals, and Tamura Ryūichi was digging trenches in Ōtsu. As for me, I had come back from Iwō Jima; having been released from the hospital I was feeling faint from malnutrition.

As if to break through this chaos, *FOU*[54] was published in October 1945. It was *Correspondence* published in magazine form by Okada Yoshihiko and his cohorts. This was the first coterie poetry magazine published after World War II. Okada wrote in its inaugural issue: "In which direction is poetry starting out? We don't know until we write."[55]

FOU was published only two months after the war ended. It is easy to see how anxious poets were to be free of the war and military oppression.

Two years later, in 1947, Kihara and some other young poets who had been early modernists in the prewar years reestablished *Arechi* (Wasteland).[56] Before the war these poets were conceptually sympathetic to the worldview expressed in T.S. Eliot's *The Waste Land*, which reflected the numbed consciousness of the population amid the

---

54. Named after a gigantic mythical bird (鵬) with a wingspan that fills the sky, said to soar to unreal heights.

55. Kihara Kōichi, "*Sengo shi monogatari*" (Tale of postwar poetry), *Eureka: shi to hihyō* (Eureka: poetry and criticism) vols. 2–13 (Tokyo: Seidosha, 1970), 180.

56. The first *Arechi* (Wasteland) was established in 1939 as a coterie magazine of young modernists with Uehara Ryūichi (who later changed his name to Ayukawa Nobuo; see footnote below) as publisher and editor. The founding members were mainly Ayukawa and his fellow college students. The final prewar issue, published in 1940, was titled *Bungei shichō* (Literary currents), in which Ayukawa stated: "Starting with this issue the title will be changed to *Literary currents*. This sixth issue is published to celebrate the 2,600th Imperial Year and our prosperous future." But he continued, "We must put new wine into new bottles and throw them far into the depths of the ocean. By and by rains that bless the land will course through the streets to change old darkness into brightness, and will nurture quiet trees amid clamour."

cityscape of post–World War I London. Now, faced with the physical destruction of their own cities and the psychological trauma of defeat, they had to deal with a total upending of their received values. The "wasteland" was their reality and truth. Ayukawa Nobuo,[57] their leader, asserted that poets must start anew by asking the fundamental question, "What is poetry?" They rejected all that belonged to the past, including their own youthful modernism, and were resolved to rise above the ruins to build their own new poetry and poetics.

At the same time, other voices that had been silenced or muted under the military regime spoke out again in full force. In 1947 *Rekitei* was reestablished. Its first post–World War II issue carried an editor's preface, dated July 1947, from Kusano Shinpei.[58]

> We hope that *Rekitei* will be crowded with poetry that can excite intelligent people of any country in the world, whatever language it might be translated into. We shall view the poetry of our country from a global vantage point, shall not belong to any factions or uphold banners as a magazine, and dedicate ourselves to poetry itself.[59]

Once again poets were setting their sights on broader and more distant horizons. *Rekitei* maintains its inclusive editorial policy to this day, continuing to publish a wide spectrum of poetry. *Shiki* was also revived, but did not do well in the postwar environment. Many small coterie poetry magazines also arose all over Japan, providing forums for widely diverse kinds of writers. Some were determined to create their own new poetics and aesthetics from the ground up, while others focused their energies on social concerns or the rebuilding of a vision of humanity in the rapidly changing postwar world.

---

57. Ayukawa Nobuo (1920–1986) was a poet, translator, and literary theorist and critic. Ayukawa published more than a dozen books of his own poetry and criticism. His translations include poetry of T.S. Eliot.

58. Kusano Shinpei (1903–1988) was a poet, editor, and translator of poetry. After dropping out of high school, he studied at a university in China, where he tried to translate English and American poetry and wrote poetry of his own, while encountering anarchistic literature. He was a founding member of *Rekitei* (Journey).

59. Ōoka, *Shōwa shishi*, 129.

FOUR POETS AFTER THE WAR

For three years after the end of the war Murō Saisei continued to live in the mountains, where he and his family had taken refuge from the Tokyo air raids. His prewar works were back in print and his poetry remained popular with the general public. But times had changed, and the younger generation was pursuing a new poetics. The postwar poetry scene was not receptive to the lyrical poetry of the past. He fell silent for years, but still enjoyed widespread respect and recognition not only as an elder poet but as a popular novelist. He was named a member of the Japan Academy of Arts in 1948. A decade after the war ended, he again started to produce spectacularly popular novels, but published only one new book of poems, titled *Kinō irasshitte kudasai* (Please come yesterday, 1959), in which he writes poems as dramatic dialogues between a man and a woman. In 1962 he published a completely reedited collection of his past books of poetry, which he had long wanted to do. A month later he died at seventy-four. He left behind a depressive poem, posthumously released, likening himself to a prawn in despair,[60] which seems to express his state of mind as a poet in his last years.

Miyoshi Tatsuji also continued to be very popular among the reading public. But the stark contrast between his wartime poetry in praise of Japan's reported or anticipated victories and his postwar essays criticizing the military and calling for the Emperor to be held responsible for the war elicited scathing attacks on his integrity, poetry, and lyricism from younger poets, notably Ayukawa Nobuo, the leader of the *Arechi* group. Because they saw Miyoshi as a driving force in shaping and promoting lyrical poetry as editor of *Shiki*, they categorically rejected not only Miyoshi and his work, but also the magazine and the lyricism associated with it. The judgmental intolerance of these young poets was fueled in part by their determination to break from the aesthetics of the past. Miyoshi's sustained popularity among general

---

60. "Song of an Old Prawn," *Murō Saisei, Nihon shijin zenshū 15* (Murō Saisei: Complete collection of Japanese poets vol. 15) (Tokyo: Shinchōsha, 1971), 196.

readers and his elevated position in the circle of established poets no doubt also played a role in energizing their self-righteous rejection.

In spite of this antipathy Miyoshi published a number of books of original and selected poems, coauthored a selection of Tang dynasty Chinese poetry, and published books of essays. In 1953 the Japan Academy of Arts honored him with an award for his lifetime of work in poetry. While Miyoshi's lyrical poems remained popular among readers, it took decades for literary critics to discuss his work impartially due to unresolved issues surrounding the wartime responsibilities of writers. When Miyoshi published *Teihon Miyoshi Tatsuji zenshishū* (Authorized complete poems of Miyoshi Tatsuji) in 1962, he excluded most of his poems in praise of war. The book was given the Yomiuri Literary Award in 1963, the same year he was named a member of the Japan Academy of Arts. He passed away in 1964 at the age of sixty-four.

Kaneko Mitsuharu, like Murō Saisei, had taken shelter in the mountains from the Tokyo air raids. He and his wife waited a year before returning to the war-torn city. In the postwar world of democracy and free speech, he decided to publish his antiwar poetry in a few volumes, and then to get on with his new life. In 1948 and 1949, Kaneko published *Rakkasan* (Parachute), *Ga* (Moths), and *Oni no ko no uta* (Songs of the ogre's children), which collected poems he had written from the 1930s through the end of the war. The intensity of indignation that had propelled his antiwar and antiregime poetry before and during the war years was then redirected to observations of the chaotic postwar period, deepening his insight into humanity. He energetically wrote and published new books of poetry and essays. He also actively participated in discourses with younger poets on poetry, poetics, and current affairs. In the newly free world he was finally recognized as a major poet of twentieth-century Japan, receiving the Yomiuri Literary Prize in 1952 for *Ningen no higeki* (Tragedy of man). His rebellious spirit, along with his objective and principled views of humanity and its destiny, remained constant until his death in 1975.

Nagase Kiyoko had quietly but steadily built a career as a poet in the prewar and wartime years. In mid-August 1945, only days after the defeat in the war was announced, Nagase was already preparing to establish a coterie magazine with her fellow poets. Postwar democracy brought with it freedom of speech and the recognition of women's rights, creating an entirely new environment with increased opportunities for her as a woman and a poet. She wrote prolifically and published in poetry magazines all over Japan, published books of poetry, and took on the chairpersonship of the local women's association. She was awarded the first Okayama Prefecture Cultural Award.

Soon Nagase became a nationally admired poet, giving lectures and readings beyond Okayama and mentoring aspiring young poets who visited her for advice and inspiration. In 1952 she and six other women initiated a women's coterie magazine, of which Nagase edited 123 issues through 1987. Concurrently she won an elected office in the board of education, and became involved in women's issues, the peace movement, and social inequality issues. In 1955 she attended the Conference of Asian Countries in India, representing her local women's association, which gave her the opportunity for a two month tour of India and China. From 1963 to 1977 she served as acting director, Secretariat of the Okayama Council of the World Federation of Nations, her first regular job. In spite of these demands on her time she published new books of poetry, aphorisms, and essays, while contributing to local publications and major national poetry magazines. In addition to two books of poetry published before the end of World War II, Nagase produced nine books of poetry, six books of selected poems, three books of aphorisms, and several books of essays between 1946 and her death on her eighty-ninth birthday in 1995. In the intervening years she received numerous awards for her poetry and her contributions to the community, including recognition as a Pioneer Poet by the Japan Poets' Association in 1982.

POSTWAR POETS

Poetry written after 1945 and into the 1960s is generally classified as *sengoshi* (postwar poetry), another subset of modern Japanese poetry. Ōoka Makoto, in his *Tōji no kakei* (A prodigal son's descendants),[61] gives an insightful mapping of the postwar poetry scene through his vantage point of being a participant as a prominent poet and of being a keen observer as a literary critic. Ōoka sees three distinct generational groups in the postwar poetry. The first generation of postwar poets, such as those in the *Arechi* group, were already young aspiring writers in the 1940s, including Ayukawa Nobuo, *Arechi*'s leader, and Tamura Ryūichi,[62] who exemplified its poetic concepts in his work. Many of them were drafted, sent to war zones, lost friends in the war, and witnessed the physical devastation of their homeland. Their uniquely introspective poetry and poetics came out of their war experience. They felt the need to reject the old world order, and resolved to rise from the rubble and create a new poetic world of their own. These are the poets to whose work the term *sengoshi* is most applicable.

The second generation of postwar poets were those born in the early 1930s, who entered the poetry scene in the 1950s. They too were exposed to wartime education, but were too young to be drafted. Even though they were spared the immediate experience of war, they had to face an abrupt change from the prewar world order to the democracy-based education they received as teenagers. Yet, reflecting the brighter world view prevalent in a Japan on its way to full recovery, they were in general more open, curious, and individualistic than the first *sen-*

---

61. Ōoka Makoto, "Sengoshi gaikan" (Overview of postwar modern Japanese poetry), in *Tōji no kakei: nihon gendaishi no ayumi* (A prodigal son's descendants: Evolution of modern Japanese poetry) (Tokyo: Shichōsha, 1969), 146–280.

62. Tamura Ryūichi (1923–1998) was a masterful poet and prolific writer of essays, and a translator of British and American mystery novels. Ayukawa Nobuo called him the "pilot" of the *Arechi* group. His powerful poetry is devoid of lyricism, philosophically astute, and stylistically unique. His many awards for his poetry include the Takamura Kōtarō Award for his book *Kotoba no nai sekai* (World without words) (Tokyo: Shōrinsha, 1962).

goshi generation. This generation of poets includes Tanikawa Shuntarō[63] and Ōoka Makoto.

The third generation of postwar poets was born after 1935. Too young to be influenced by wartime education, they were free to explore new directions in poetry. They include Suzuki Shirōyasu[64] and Yoshimasu Gōzō,[65] both of whom are radical innovators conceptually and linguistically, and are known for creating multimedia poetic experiences. These three generations have produced a remarkably varied body of work, and their younger successors continue to push the boundaries of the art in contemporary Japan.

---

63. Tanikawa Shuntarō (1931–) is indisputably the most widely read poet in Japan, and has a substantial recognition internationally. He has published over sixty critically acclaimed volumes of poetry, along with numerous books on poetry and poetics, dialogues with experts outside the field of literature, children's books, and rhythmic word games. He received the first Hagiwara Sakutarō Award for *Seken shirazu* (Clueless) in 1993, among many other honors.

64. Suzuki Shirōyasu (1935–) is a poet and creator in cinematic art and design. Since the 1960s he has pioneered in producing poetry that is a radical departure from the cultural norms of the time in its diction, images, and messages. Along with poetry, for which he has received a number of prestigious awards, he has produced many photo, video, and film creations.

65. Yoshimasu Gōzō (1939–) is a prolific poet, photographer, and multimedia creative artist. While his earlier poems are known for their radically fresh, rhythmic, speedy, and daring verbiage, he later incorporated music and beats with words. He also collaborates with musicians and dancers to present a totally unique world of multimedia art. His many honors and awards include his first, the first Takami Jun Award for *Ōgon shihen* (Golden poems) in 1970 and the 2003 Medal with Purple Ribbon from the Japanese government.

MURŌ SAISEI
室生犀星

Murō Saisei
(1889–1962)

LIFE AND CAREER

Verbalizing his feelings must have been cathartic for Murō Saisei, for he wrote prolifically as a haiku poet, modern poet, and best-selling novelist. Fortunately, at every point in his career when he sought a new direction, he met someone who recognized his genius and provided opportunities for him to demonstrate his creativity.

Born to a sixty-four-year-old former retainer for a feudal lord and a thirty-four-year-old household maid in Kanazawa on the Japan Sea coast, Murō was adopted by the head priest of a local temple and raised by him and his common-law wife. His biological father died when he was ten, and his birth mother was dismissed and disappeared following his father's death. His adoptive mother often brought up the "shameful" nature of his birth. He later described his childhood as tragic for himself and his birth mother.

Murō entered elementary school a semester late, probably due to his adoptive mother's negligence.[1] A lonely and defiant child, rough and unmannerly, unpopular among fellow pupils and teachers, he spent a great deal of time alone on the bank of the river Sai, taking solace in the beauty of nature. Saisei, his pen-name, is written with two ideograms 犀星: "Sai," the name of the river, and "sei," meaning stars. He dropped out of school at thirteen, and started working as an errand boy in the Kanazawa district court. He had to hand all his pay over to his adoptive mother.

---

1. Murō, *Shijin zenshū* 15, 321.

Encouraged by his manager at work, Kawakami Fūkotsu, who was a haiku poet, he started composing haiku when he was fourteen, which "allowed the mind and heart of [my] youthful days to flow out fully." He said Fūkotsu was "the only person I could call my master in my entire life."[2] He was introduced to a local group of haiku practitioners, welcomed and appreciated as a talented youth. His submissions to a local newspaper haiku forum were accepted. In 1905, at seventeen years of age, he created a magazine for circulation among his coworkers at the court and wrote haiku, compositions, and editor's notes for it. He also wrote New Style poetry that he submitted to the poetry magazine *Shinsei* (New voices). *Shinsei* not only published his poems but named them the best of the year's submissions. This prompted him to think of pursuing poetry seriously.

Burning with desire to be a poet, and anxious to be at the center of the poetry world, Murō set off for Tokyo for the first time in 1910, carrying only his poems, some blank paper, and a walking stick. He hoped to meet the poets and editors he admired. But he found himself working as legal scribe in the basement of Tokyo District Court for subsistence wages while writing poetry every day. The following summer, unable to cope with Tokyo's heat and his own poverty, he had to return to Kanazawa. Murō called the poems he wrote around these days lyrical songs, and toward the end of his life, he commented on these lyrical poems in retrospect as poetry that "finally depicts the world of desolation divorced from poetic elegance."[3] This was a clear departure from the romantic lyricism of early modern Japanese poetry, a revolutionary achievement that upon publication impressed and excited contemporary poets and novelists alike.

When Kitahara Hakushū read Murō's lyrical poems he published two of them in the January 1913 issue of *ZAMBOA* and included his poems in all subsequent issues until the magazine ceased publication in May of that year. His appearances in *ZAMBOA* gained him considerable renown in poetry circles. Hagiwara Sakutarō was so impressed

---

2. Ibid., 323.

3. Murō Saisei, *Murō Saisei zenshishū* (Complete poems of Murō Saisei) (Tokyo: Chikumashobō, 1962), 596.

with Murō's poems that he wrote an enthusiastic letter of admiration, which triggered a lasting friendship between the two poets. It should be noted that Hagiwara was himself a formidable lyrical poet and theorist,[4] but called Murō his mentor. In 1916 Murō and Hagiwara established Kanjō shisha (Sentiments Poetry Press), through which they published the magazine *Kanjō* (Sentiments). In its July and August issues, *Kanjō* featured sixty of Murō's short lyrical poems under the title of "selected lyrical songs."

In 1918 *Ai no shishū* (Poems of love), which contained poems written between 1915 and 1918, was published through Kanjō shisha. All 550 copies of *Ai no shishū* sold out in one month, bringing him his first paycheck as a poet. Later in the year he published a collection of lyrical poems as *Jojō shōkyoku shū* (Lyrical songs), which contained poems he wrote around 1909 to 1911. These books propelled Murō to the center of the modern lyrical poetry movement, attracting many poets to gather at his home. His poetry had a strong influence on the next generation of lyrical poets, such as Hori Tatsuo, Nakano Shigeharu, and Miyoshi Tatsuji.

After the publication of *Daini ai no shishū* (Poems of love II) in 1919, Murō felt he had accomplished what he had so fervently wanted to do and had "nothing left in him for poetry."[5] Yet he continued to write poetry and haiku, while pouring his energy into learning how to compose novels. During the following year he wrote a number of novels, though he also published the book of poems *Sabishiki tokai* (Lonely city). His work won him the 1928 Watanabe Prize, a prestigious literary prize awarded to promising new writers by the Japan Writers' Association.

Although Murō continued to produce novels during the 1930s and into the war years, along with his fourteen-volume collected works, he published nine books of poetry. In 1937 he toured Manchuria for a month, the only time he travelled outside Japan, but he never wrote anything in support of Japan's colonialist initiatives of the time.

---

4. Hagiwara Sakutarō, *Principles of Poetry (Shi no genri)*, translated by C.I. Wang and Isamu P. Fukuchi (Ithaca, NY: Cornell East Asia Program, 1998).

5. Murō, *Shijin zenshū 15*, 327.

During the war years his creative output was dominated by prose works with aristocratic themes associated with the elegance of a distant past. He asserted that writers should continue writing even during the war and published two books of poetry and a dozen novels as well as stories for children and young girls. He also edited *Satō Sōnosuke shishū* (Collected poems of Satō Sōnosuke).[6] As the air raids on Tokyo intensified in 1944, he moved to the resort village of Karuizawa with his family, where he remained until late 1949.

Publishing activities in Japan, suspended during the last year of World War II, resumed right after the war ended. Despite the hardships and privations of the postwar period, the reading public was eager for stories and poetry, and demand for Murō's work was high. Seventeen of his books were reprinted in 1946 and 1947 alone.

Murō's total output included over twenty books of poetry and four major collections of haiku, but most of this work dates from the prewar years. While he had a spectacular career as a best-selling, award-winning novelist after the war, and retained his reputation as a master poet, the only book of new poetry he produced was *Kinō irasshitte kudasai* (Please come back yesterday), published in 1959. His 1957 book, *Harubin shishū* (Ha'erbin poems), contained poems he had written in 1937, when he went to Ha'erbin, China, and toured the vast steppes of Manchuria.

By any measure Murō would seem to have had a remarkably successful and fulfilling career. He was a distinguished poet, a popular author of highly regarded fiction, and a respected essayist. Few writers excel in so many genres or wield as much influence as he did. Yet all this renown does not seem to have brought him satisfaction, as seen in his poem "Song of an Old Prawn," written a month before his death in 1962.

---

6. See footnote 36 in Introduction. Satō Sōnosuke was a brilliant poet, and Nagase Kiyoko's mentor.

POETRY

Composing poems was a serious, intense process for Murō, an arduous task in which he sought to meet and capture the inspiration that welled up within him. Much later in life he pointed out that Basho, in an effort to establish his style of haiku, "travelled for two long months, as far back as two hundred years ago, which meant he bet his life on it."[7] So did Murō on his poetry. When he looked back at his career, which began with the publication of *Ai no shishū* (Poems of love), he declared that "everything seemed fresh to my eyes, and in my youthful season I was discovering things I had missed when I saw them first; behind them lyrical poetry was already there, swirling. I staked almost the entirety of my life on it. The fact that I did not step out of the world of lyrical poetry throughout my career is something I can be proud of, and I did not make a mistake in my choice."[8]

His lyrical poetry expresses the depths of a solitary heart, seen against the backdrop of nature, which deeply touched the readers of his time. Even today, in very different social and economic circumstances, it is very affecting. His poems share what "swirls" in the depths of the heart, elevating a poet's personal experience into one that transcends time and space. In the 1920s his poetry displayed an increasing urgency in the pursuit of his art, with a focus on capturing something real, yet hidden and unknown to him. The poet keeps up with that pursuit even though it seems futile, as shown in "What I See Inside Myself." This poem depicts a mindscape oppressed by an intensely visual, audible, and tactile inner experience that invites readers to share the speaker's feeling of urgency.

Predominating other sensory information, the sights and sounds of nature were the dominant components of Murō's poetry throughout his career. For example, "Lonely Spring" opens with auditory and visual cues that conjure up a feeling of deep melancholy on a quiet and slow spring day spent beside a turning waterwheel in the countryside.

---

7. Murō, "Shi e no kokubetsu ni tsuite Hagiwara-kun ni kotahu" (Response to Hagiwara regarding departure from poetry), in Murō, *Shijin zenshū 15*, 270.

8. Murō, *Zenshishū*, 595.

The first line reads "The sunlight softly drips on and on." The verb in this line conveys the gentle dripping of liquid, and when we first read this poem we may wonder how sunlight could drip, and why it is so like water. Then we realize that the waterwheel is lifting some water as it turns slowly in the sun. Water droplets, bathed in light and falling off the wheel, gently shine as if each drop of water is sunlight itself. We hear the water and see the sunlight dripping at the pace of the wheel lazily turning in a stream. Murō is using the essential element of haiku technique, which is to capture observations and sensory experiences in a few intuitive images, and inviting readers to deeper insight and more complex layers of meaning.

Murō's voice changed in tone and color over his long career. The intense emotions he expressed were internalized and subjective in his earlier poems. Later, however, his voice gained objectivity and his eyes turned more toward observation of the reality surrounding him, as we see in "A Valley at Surugadai." This poem paints a corner of Tokyo as a deserted urban valley where he lives but finds no consolation, where nature is far away and simple survival is the paramount issue. In "The Temple," back in his hometown, his voice is cool and almost indifferent. He accepts the reality of the changes that time has brought to the temple where he grew up. His detachment is even more striking in "Look at This Man" when he comes upon an aged acquaintance who no longer recognizes him. There is a vast gulf between this disengaged observer and the fresh voice of "Morning Song" that celebrates joy and peace. It is as if Murō had lost the urgency, spark, and excitement of inspiration and discovery conveyed in his early poems. That might explain his declaration that he was parting from poetry at the height of his poetic career (even though he continued to write it). Given the fact, however, that his declaration appeared toward the end of the 1920s, when the literary world saw the rise of proletarian poety while the Peace Preservation Law was increasingly expanding its reach to control freedom of speech, one wonders if it reflected Murō's despair in sensing the approaching end of honest expression in creative activities.

In terms of his post–World War II poetry, Murō seemingly remained skeptical. "Three Years in the Mountains," for example, deals with his departure from nature and its eternal self-renewal in the mountains where he had taken shelter from wartime air raids. In his original version, which is included in this book, he expressed his commitment, as a survivor, to remember friends who had lost their lives in the war. Murō, in his last years, significantly revised this piece for his *zenshishū* (complete poems), cutting out the whole section after the line "look" in the middle of the poem. It is impossible to guess his motivation for changing a thoughtful tribute to the victims of the war into a simple leave-taking from the mountains. One wonders if Murō was trying to obliterate the memories of the senseless war.

"The River Sai" is also presented in its original form in this book, instead of the truncated version of his final rewrite. The shorter rewritten version reads: "There flowed a lovely river / I was born by the river / I would sit on its flowering bank / Among spring flowers in spring / Summer bridges [sic] in summer / And open the feelings of storybooks." It omits the specific stimuli that inspired the poet.

Murō's last book of poems, *Kinō irasshitte kudasai* (Please come yesterday, 1959), marks a new and final phase of his poetry. Taken as a whole, the poems in this book constitute a sketch for a play about an affair between a man and a woman. Their relationship develops from casual encounter to being lovers, and ends with the woman leaving. The tone is sardonic, ironic, inquisitive, or daringly sexual by turns. The book reads like a script for a modern verse play, presenting a woman who remains standoffish and scornful of the man, and a man who cannot help but be physically attracted to her.

Murō's style and diction were straightforward and forthright throughout his career. His poetry is crisp and to the point, using the language and rhythms of ordinary speech. His determination to grapple with his subject matter head-on is reinforced by the economy of his language, which is akin to the method of haiku. In the end, Murō's stature as a great modern poet rests on his lyricism expressed in a manner "divorced from the poetic elegance" of the past, as Murō himself notes.

はる

おれがいつも詩を書いてゐると
永遠がやつて来て
ひたひに何か知らなすつて行く
手をやつて見るけれど
すこしのあとも残さない素早い奴だ
おれはいつもそいつを見ようとして
あせつては手を焼いてゐる
時がだんだん進んで行く
おれの心にしみを遺して
おれのひたひを何時もひりひりさせて行く
けれどもおれは詩をやめない
おれはやはり街から街をあるいたり
泥濘にはまつたりしてゐる

愛の詩集　*Ai no shi shū*

SPRING

Every time I write a poem
Eternity comes by and
Brushes my forehead with something
But he is so swift that there's nothing left
By the time I try to touch it
Each time I desperately struggle to see him
But in vain
Time ticks on
Leaving stains on my heart
Leaving my forehead smarting
Still I would not give up poetry
I'd still walk from one town to another
or fall into the mud

1918. *Poems of love*

朝の歌

こどものやうな美しい気がして
けさは朝はやく起きて出た
日はうらうらと若い木木のあたまに
すがらしい光をみなぎらしてゐた
こどもらは喜ばしい朝のうたをうたってゐた
その澄んだこゑは
おれの静かな心にしみ込んで来た
何といふ美しい朝であらう

愛の詩集　*Ai no shi shū*

MORNING SONG

Feeling lovely as a child
I awoke early this morning and came outside
The sun gently crowned the tops of young trees
With its abundant refreshing light
Children were singing happy morning songs
Their clear voices
Reached into my serene heart
What a lovely morning

1918. *Poems of love*

故郷にて冬を送る

ある日たうどう冬が来た
たしかに来た
鳴りひびいて
海鳴りは昼の間も空をあるいてゐた
自分はからだに力を感じた
木は根をくみ合せ
落葉は空に舞ひ上った
冬の意識はしんとした一時にも現はれた
自分は目を挙げて
悲しさうに街区を眺めた
礑には一面に水が鋭く走ってゐた

愛の詩集　*Ai no shi shū*

Winter in My Hometown

One day, at last, Winter came
Surely it arrived
Resounding
the sea's roar roamed in the sky in daylight too
I felt its power within myself
Trees knotted their roots
Dry leaves danced up into the sky
Winter's spirit emerged even in the quiet
I raised my eyes
To survey the city streets with sadness
Water was racing fiercely over the riverbed

1918. *Poems of love*

ドストエフスキイの肖像

深大なる素朴
耐へ忍んだ永い苦しみ
鈍い歩調で迫る君の精神
そのひたひには
ペテルブルグの汚れた空気が
くもの巣のやうにかかってゐる
騒音がする
叫びが聞える
悩んだものの美がある
強いねんばりした人間性
ねちねちした生命
肩はばの広い　おこりっぽいやうな此の人
この人は迫る
温かい呼吸で迫る
あなたは貧乏に打勝った
あなたはシベリアの監獄に四年も居た
あなたの葬式に露西亜の大学生が
その棺のあとから
鎖や手錠を曳いて
参詣しょうとして官憲から停められた
この堪へがたい愚鈍なやうな顔
精神の美しさにみなぎった顔
何を為てゐたか　伝記学者も
解らないこの人の暗黒時代
此の人の前で勉強をし
我慢に我慢をかさね勉強をすること
誓へ
ほんとによく生き
よく勉強してゆくことを

愛の詩集　*Ai no shi shū*

A Portrait of Dostoyevsky

profound simplicity
long suffering endured
your spirit plods over to me
around your brow
St. Petersburg's stale air
hangs like a spider web
I hear noises
I hear screams
I see the beauty of one who's gone through suffering
a man of tough tenacious humanity
of dogged life
with broad shoulders, irritable
you come upon me
upon me with warm breath
you overpowered poverty
you were jailed in Siberia for four long years
at your funeral Russian university students tried to pay respects
following your coffin, dragging their handcuffs and chains,
but the authorities stopped them
your face, irresistibly idiotlike
your face, brimming with spiritual beauty
even your biographers don't know
what you were doing during your dark times
I swear before you:
I will learn
I will persevere and endure and learn
to truthfully live a good life
and continue to learn

1918. *Poems of love*

抒情小曲集　序曲

芽がつつ立つ
ナイフのやうな芽が
たつた一本
すつきりと蒼空(あをぞら)につつ立つ

抒情小曲集　*Jojō shōkyoku shū*

Lyrical Songs: Prelude

A shoot stands straight up
like a knife
the single shoot
slim points into the blue sky

1918. *Lyrical songs*

犀川

うつくしき川は流れたり
そのほとりに我は住みぬ
春は春、なつはなつの
花つける堤に坐りて
こまやけき本のなさけと愛とを知りぬ
いまもその川のながれ
美しき微風ととも
蒼き波たたへたり

抒情小曲集　*Jojō shōkyoku shū*

The River Sai

There flowed a lovely river
I used to live by the river
I would sit on its flowering bank
Among spring flowers in spring
Summer flowers in summer
And came to know storybook intricacies of emotion and love
The river still flows on
Along with gentle breezes
Brimming with blue ripples

1918. *Lyrical songs*

寂しき春

したたり止まぬ日のひかり
うつうつまはる水ぐるま
あをぞらに
越後の山も見ゆるぞ
さびしいぞ

一日もの言はず
野にいでてあゆめば
菜種のはなのだんだんは
遠いあなたに波をつくりて
いまははや　やむごともなく
しんにさびしいぞ

抒情小曲集　*Jojō shōkyoku shū*

LONELY SPRING

The sunlight gently drips on
The waterwheel turns, listless
Against the blue sky
I see the Echigo mountain ridges, distant
I am lonely

Not uttering a word all day
I am out in the field to take a walk
Terraces of mustard flowers
Form waves into the far beyond
Now I am so inconsolably
deeply
lonely

1918. *Lyrical songs*

砂丘の上

渚には蒼き波のむれ
かもめのごとくひるがへる
過ぎし日はうすあをく
海のかなたに死にうかぶ
おともなく砂丘の上にうづくまり
海のかなたを恋ひぬれて
ひとりただひとり
はるかにおもひつかれたり

抒情小曲集　*Jojō shōkyoku shū*

On a Sand Dune

Blue waves frolic at the water's edge
Flipping like seagulls
Past days, pale blue
Float lifeless far out to the sea
I squat silently on a sand dune
Yearning in despair for someplace beyond the sea
Alone all alone
I am tired of this distant longing

1918. *Lyrical songs*

小さい家庭

僕はいま小さい家庭をつくりかけてゐる
まるで小鳥の巣に似たやうなものを
自分は毎日
二つの心を持ち合って
一枚のまづしい蓆を編むやうに
たてとよことの糸を縒り合せてゐる
自分はこの小さい家庭を愛する
暁明がくるとともに
ぱちぱち燃える薪の音がする
空では星がきえ初める
僕は起き出てそれに従ふ
この世の愉快なくるしいどよみに従ふ
書物はみな一つ一つに呼吸をして
あついペエジの羽ばたきをやる
妻は木綿の朝のきものをきて
もう猛り立つ犬と庭で遊んでゐる
僕もその仲間にはいる
犬は高く高く吠え猛って
朝の挨拶をする

第二愛の詩集　*Dai ni ai no shi shū*

A Small Home

I am now building a small home
I bring two hearts together
every day
to weave something like a bird's nest
like a single meager straw mat
of entwined warp and weft
I love this small home
As the day breaks
I hear the sputtering flames of a wood fire
Stars begin to fade from the sky
I rise and keep pace with them
I follow the noises of the world, both happy and painful
Every book breathes on its own
beating the wings of thick pages
My wife, in her cotton morning robe
is already playing with our fiercely excited dog
I join them
The dog barks louder and louder
saying his morning greetings

1919. *Poems of love II*

音楽会の後

人人の心はかなり深くつかれて
濡れてでもゐるやうに
愉しいさざなみを打ってゐた
人人は音楽が語る言葉の微妙さについて囁いてゐた
階段から芝生に
芝生の下萌えをふんで
もはや街燈のついた公園の方へ歩いてゐた
美しい妹をもつひと
たのしい女の友をもつひと
妻をもつひと
それらはみな一様な疲れのうちに
ふしぎと生き生きした昂奮を抱いて歩いてゐた
私もそれらの群のあとにつづいて
寂しい自分の靴音を感じながら
春近い公園の方をあるいてゐた

第二愛の詩集　*Dai ni ai no shi shū*

After a Concert

Deeply touched
People's hearts rippled with joy
As if drenched
People whispering about Music's subtle language
Walked from the stairs to the lawn
Treading on the young grass
Toward the park where the lamps were already lit
Those who had adorable sisters
Those who had delightful girl friends
Those who had wives
They, in their shared languor,
All embraced a mystifying spirited excitement
I walked in their trail
With the lonely sound of my own shoes
In the park nearing spring

1919. *Poems of love II*

みな休息して

夕方になると
白いかもめの群が
隅田川の方を指して渡ってゆく
空の澄んだ日に
くっきりと浮彫りにされて
優しいつばさの音まで
はたはたときこえて来る
毎日のやうに規則正しく
夕方になるとそれが見られる
いつも一日の仕事が終って
庭で休むとき
はたはたと渡ってゆくのを見る

第二愛の詩集　*Dai ni ai no shi shū*

All in Repose

As the evening arrives
a flock of white seagulls
flies above toward the Sumida River
On a fine day
they are sharply carved against the clear sky
I can even hear their graceful wings
gently wave
Almost every day, regularly
I see them in the evening
When I rest in the yard
after a day's work
I see them fly across the sky waving

1919. *Poems of love II*

曙光を目ざして

私は日没に近く一羽の鳥が
矢のやうに空を駛るのを見た
まるで火のやうだ

かれの渡った空間には
もはや一日の終りが
かの巨大な暗黒とともに初まってゐた
しかし何事も起らない此の暗黒の涯に
かれは今何の光輝を見いだしたのだ

火よりも迅く
一羽の鳥が駛る

第二愛の詩集　*Dai ni ai no shi shū*

Aiming at the First Light of Dawn

Near sunset I saw a bird
flash through the sky like an arrow
like fire

In the space he crossed
the end of the day had already begun
with a familiar mass of darkness
But what glory did he find
at the edge of this darkness where nothing is happening?

Swifter than fire
a bird flashed by

1919. *Poems of love II*

燃える

烈しい寒ざらしのかぜのふく朝
ゆきずりに美しいものを見た
どこの女かしらない
寒さにさらしつくされたやうな頬をして
真赤にほてらして
ちからをあるだけの肉体(からだ)にこめ
とつとつと歩いてゆくのだ
その頬は実際燃えてゐる
寒風なんぞは何んでもなく見える
風のほうでもみな反れてゆく
とてもかなはないらしく

寂しき都会　*Sabishiki tokai*

Aflame

One morning when a fierce winter wind was raging
I saw beauty in passing
I don't know who she was
With her cheeks glowing a flaming red
Totally exposed to the cold
She gathered all her strength
And determinedly walked on
Her cheeks were actually aflame
They seemed to dismiss the cold wind as nothing
The wind also veered away from her
It seemed no match for her

1920. *Lonely city*

夜半

みな花をもて飾りしひつぎをばとりまき
あめふる夜半(よは)をすごしぬ
人の世のちひさき魂をなぐさめんと
けぶれる青い草のやうなるせん香を
たえまなくささげたりけり
その座にわれもありまづしき父おやとして
そだちがたきものをそだてんと
日夜のつかれ我もつらなりぬ

忘春詩集　*Bōshun shi shū*

In the Dead of Night

Surrounding the coffin covered with flowers
Everyone stayed up through the rainy night
To console your soul young in life
Incense was ceaselessly offered
Like a smoldering green blade
I was also among them as a poor father
Who tried to raise you as you struggled to survive
I sat fatigued from our efforts day and night

1922. *Poems of lost spring*

靴下

毛糸にて編める靴下をもはかせ
好めるおもちゃをも入れ
あみがさ　わらぢのたぐひをもをさめ
石をもてひつぎを打ち
かくて野に出でゆかしめぬ

おのれ父たるゆゑに
野辺の送りをすべきものにあらずと
われひとり留まり
庭などをながめあるほどに
耐へがたくなり
煙草を噛みしめにけり

忘春詩集　*Bōshun shi shū*

The Socks

I also put a pair of knit woolen socks on your feet
placed your favorite toys by you
and included a straw hat and sandals for your travel
We nailed the coffin with a stone
Thus we sent you off to burial

Because I am your father
I was not allowed at your burial
I stayed back alone
looking out at the yard
Unable to bear it all
I sank my teeth into a cigarette

1922. *Poems of lost spring*

我が家の花

そとより帰りきたれば
ちひさきおもちゃの包みかかへ
いそいそとして我が家の門をくぐりしが
いまそのちひさき我が子みまかり
われを迎へいづるものなし
母おやはつねにしづかにしづかにと言ひ
あかごの目のさめんことをおそれぬ
さればわれはその癖づきし足もとを静め
そとより格子をあくればとて
もはや眠らん子どもとてなし
かくして我が家の花散りゆけり

忘春詩集　*Bōshun shi shū*

The Flower of My Family

I used to come home
Holding a small package of toys in my arms
I would walk through the gate with excitement
Now my little child has been taken away and
No one meets me

His mother used to hush me to be quiet
Worried about surprising our baby
As I have trained myself
I quietly slide open the latticed front door
But we have no sleeping baby anymore
The flower of my family has fallen away

1922. *Poems of lost spring*

春の寺

うつくしきみ寺なり
み寺にさくられうらんたれば
うぐひすしたたり
さくら樹にすずめら交(さか)り
かんかんと鐘鳴りてすずろなり
かんかんと鐘鳴りてさかんなれば
をとめらひそやかに
ちちははのなすことをして遊ぶなり
門もくれなゐ炎炎と
うつくしき春のみ寺なり

青き魚を釣る人　*Aoki uo o tsuru hito*

The Temple in Spring

The temple is lovely
Cherry blossoms are massively abundant
Bush-warblers call intermittently
Sparrows mate among the cherry trees
The temple bell sounds appealing
As the temple bell appealingly resonates
Girls quietly play
Doing what their mothers and fathers do
The gate is also crimson, aflame
The temple is in spring's splendor

1923. *The man fishing blue fish*

山なみ

うれしや
ふるさとに自動車がしなをつくりて
鋭(と)き山なみのもとを過ぎゆきぬ。
山より月のぼりいで
われらがうへに瑠璃(るり)をはりつむる。
君にこよひこそ
わが思ひあかさむ。

青き魚を釣る人　*Aoki uo o tsuru hito*

Mountains

How blissful
In my hometown automobiles flirtingly
Move along the foothills of the rugged mountains
The moon rises from the mountains
And covers us with blue jewels
Tonight, at last, I will reveal
My heart to you

1923. *The man fishing blue fish*

雪くる前

ひとすぢに逢ひたさの迫りて
酢のごとく烈しきもの
胸ふかく走りすぐるときなり
雪くると呼ばはるこゑす
はやくも白くはなりし屋根の上

青き魚を釣る人　*Aoki uo o tsuru hito*

Before the Snow

The acute desire to see her comes over me
Something as searing as acid
Pierces deep through my heart
I hear voices warning of snow
Rooftops are already white

1923. *The man fishing blue fish*

己の中に見ゆ

我はくろがねの扉の前に佇めり
我はひねもす其扉を噛じれり
或は爪をもって引掻き穴をあけんとせり
くろがねの扉に血のごときもの垂れたり
その響は聾するごとし
我は飽くことなくその扉を叩けり
動かざるものを動かさむとはせり
扉の奥に何物のあらんや
何物を得んとするや
我は恐らく生涯これを叩かんとす
叩き破らんとす
身をもって耐へんとはせり

鶴　*Tsuru*

What I See Inside Myself

I linger in front of the iron door
I gnaw at the door all day long
Or try to poke a hole, scraping with my nails
Something like blood drips on the iron door
Its sound is deafening
I keep pounding at the door tirelessly
Trying to move something that will not budge
What is behind the door?
What am I trying to get?
Perhaps I will be pounding on this throughout my life
I will keep pounding till I break through
I am trying to endure with all my might

1928. *Cranes*

駿河台の谷間

みやこのそこに
いくつとなく大なる谷間ありて
つねに忘られしごとく
空より限らる
ゆるやかに舟はゆけども
もやぐべき岸辺をしらず

われパンと牛酪との包みをもち
夜食の卓につかむとして
暗然として
大なる谷間にかかる

鳥雀集　*Tori suzume shū*

A Valley at Surugadai

In the depths of the city
Are countless large valleys
Defined by the sky
As if always forgotten
Boats drift slowly
But see no shores where they can moor

With a package of bread and butter in my arms
For my supper table
I come with a gloomy heart
Upon a great valley

1930. *Birds and sparrows*

み寺

いとまありてみ寺に詣づ
み寺はあたらしく建てられ
老木のあとをとどめず
長屋のごとくみ寺はありぬ
わがそだちしみ寺はいづくぞ
獅子のごとき牡丹咲ける奥の院は
洪水にさらはれて川底にありと
詣づるひとの言へり

いにしへ　*Inishi'e*

The Temple

Having found a bit of time
I've come to the temple to pay my respects
The temple is newly built
There is no trace of aged trees
The temple stands like a tenement
Where is the temple I grew up in?
The sanctuary where a peony used to bloom like a lion?
A visitor tells me a flood took it away and
It's now in the riverbed

1943. *Times past*

帰去来

掃かんとすれど庭なく
植ゑんに木を見るすべもなし
母も父も死に絶え
えにしある人もまた絶ゆ
故山いたづらに剣のごとく立ち
残雪また夕陽に燃ゆ
帰り来つて我は去らなん

いにしへ　*Inishi'e*

I Will Leave

I would sweep the courtyard, but the courtyard is not there
There is no viewing of trees by the porch
Mother and Father have passed on
My relatives are also gone
The familiar mountain ridges soar like swords in vain
With leftover snow burning again in the setting sun
I have come back, and I will leave

1943. *Times past*

この人を見よ

この人はよく見し人なり
いまもなは生きて歩めるを見れば
古き帽子ふかぶかとかぶり
何の用あるものならん
まなこ霞めるごとく
途呆けしありさまにて行けり
ああ　この人はまだ生けりしか

いにしへ　*Inishi'e*

Look at This Man

I used to see him often
I see him still alive and on foot
With an old hat deep over his eyes
On what errand?
His eyes hazed over
His manners senile, he passes by me
Ah, he is still alive

1943. *Times past*

花

花屋に行って見たまへ
どんな花でも
色も香気も蕾も
お好み次第だ
此処で匂ふ香気をかいでゐたら
何もほしいものがなくなる
花といふものも
ぎりぎりの気特で見てゐると
その美しさは驚く外はない
花が食べものでないことは
何たる大きい徳であらう

夕映梅花　*Yūbae baika*

FLOWERS

Go visit a florist
You'll find whatever you like:
all the flowers
in any color, scent, or unopened.
As I breathe in their scent drifting here
I lose all my desire for worldly things
Flowers—
when you look at them intensely
their beauty is nothing short of a wonder
What a great virtue it is
that flowers are not food

1946. *Plum blossoms in evening glow*

鰯

鰯(いわし)があらはれた
喫驚(びっくり)したやうな眼付(めつき)で
三年ぶりで街にあらはれた
尾も折れてゐないし
あひかはらずすべすべした
はだかのままだった
深海色の背中のほくろも
大きいくろい眼はとぢることなく
瞬(またた)きもせず
天の一角を睨んでゐる

相不変(あひかはらず)お腹を悪くすると見え
海ではたらいた腹の機械は
やぶれたあばらを透いてまる見えだ
恋もしたであらうに
やぶれたお腹に風がとほる
だがしかし鰯があらはれた
まる干しが何と一びき一円
ひらいた奴が一円弐拾銭
かんかんに干せあがり
にくはしまって牛酪(バター)のごとく
皮をはいで見れば
亀甲(べっかふ)色の肌がある
海のしぶきは遠い山のうしろにある

The Sardine

The sardine is back
with a surprised look in his eyes
back in town after three years
his tail fin is intact
naked and slick as before
even his back carries moles colored like the deep seas
his large dark eyes do not close
do not blink
staring at a corner of heaven

He appears to suffer from bellyaches as always
gastric mechanisms that worked in the sea
show through his torn ribs
he must have fallen in love, too
the wind passes through his torn-up belly
but, you see, the sardine is back
goodness, one yen for a whole dried sardine
one yen and twenty-cents for a dried sardine slit open
all the sardines are perfectly sun-dried
their flesh is rich like butter
peel off the skin
and find amber-colored flesh
the splashing sea is beyond the distant mountains

汽車から下りると
駅から真直に信濃街道を
碓氷(うすひ)の屋根の雪を見ながら村に入る
草深い村には
どこにも
木々にはもはや一枚の葉も見えない
鰯の行列はしづしづと進み
木々の下を行く
木々にはみぞれと雨
どこも氷雪地帯の蕭条(せうでう)無類の冬景色だ
三年ぶりであらうか
五年ぶりだったらうか
つひに鰯があらはれた
つるつるしたはだかで。

旅びと　*Tabibito*

I get off the train
I walk straight from the station down the Shinano Trail
I enter the village looking at the snow on the Usui mountain ridges
in this remote village
not a single leaf is left on the trees
a procession of sardines solemnly goes
under the trees
tormented by sleet and rain
wherever you look
you have winter in an icebound region incomparably desolate
it's been three years?
or has it been five years?
finally the sardine is back
naked and slick.

1947. *Travelers*

三年山中

三年間僕は山中にゐたが
まなぶ自然にはてしがなく
何処にも分ったといふ結論が出ない
僕はつひに引き上げることにした
僕の命をここで棄てても
自然はまなび尽せないであらう
三十分見てをれば沢山なのに
僕は三年間山を見てゐたのだ
見てゐるうちにはるは三度も遣って来た
これではどうにも限(きり)がつかないだらう
あとから遣って来て
それを迎へてゐるひまもない
見たまへ
僕の友は戦争中にみんな亡くなった
ただひとりの友までも
あへなくなって終った
僕だけが生きのこり
うしろから送る夕栄えをけふも見る
つひに山中では僕の命は終らなかった
みやこにある僕の庭に
まなんだ自然をゑがかうとはしないが
あらはれて行けば僕はゑがくだらう
亡き友らの
かよふ小径くらゐは作れるだらう
絶えなんとしてつづく小径が
僕の机のあるところまで
僕の頭のつづくまで伸べられるだらう。

逢ひぬれば　*Ainureba*

Three Years in the Mountains

I have lived in the mountains for three years
Nature contains infinite wisdom for me to learn, but
I have yet to conclude I have truly understood any of it
I finally decided to take my leave
even if I dedicated my whole life here
I could not fathom all of Nature
a half hour of observation might have been enough
but I have been staring at the mountains for three full years
in the meantime Spring came around three times
there will be no end to this
it keeps coming around so
I hardly have time to welcome it
look
my friends all died during the war
even my closest friend
is no more
only I survived
and today too I see the evening glow sent to me from the other shore
my life did not come to an end in the mountains
I would not reproduce the Nature I have come to know
in the yard of my house in the city, but
if it appeared to me I would draw it
I could make at least
a narrow footpath my late friends could follow down to me
the tenuous trail would stretch
to where my desk is
as long as my mind can survive.

1947. *Encounters*

昨日いらつしつて下さい

きのふ　いらつしつてください
きのふの今ごろいらつしつてください
そして昨日の顔にお逢ひください
わたくしは何時も昨日の中にゐますから
きのふのいまごろなら
あなたは何でもお出来になった筈です
けれども行停りになったけふも
あすもあさっても
あなたにはもう何も用意してはございません
どうぞ　きのふに逆戻りしてください
きのふいらつしつてください
昨日へのみちはご存じの筈です
昨日の中でどうどう廻りなさいませ
その突き当りに立っていらっしゃい
突き当りが開くまで立ってゐてください
威張れるものなら威張つて立ってください

昨日いらっしってください　*Kinō irasshitte kudasai*

Please Come Back Yesterday

Please come back yesterday
Come about this time yesterday
And meet the face of yesterday
Because I am always inside yesterday
You could do anything
If it were around this time yesterday
But today when your path is blocked
Or tomorrow or the day after
I have nothing ready for you
Please, go back to yesterday
Come yesterday
You should know the path to yesterday
Go around and round inside yesterday
Just keep standing at the dead end
Keep standing until the dead end opens
If you dare to stand on your dignity, stand with your dignity

1959. *Please come back yesterday*

誰かに

誰かに逢ひ
話をしかけられた
くらい中であった
何かの中心に私はゐた
誰かに逢へる予感はくづれ
誰かはすぐに去って了った
つまらないただの女であった
女は長い赤いきれを引きずり
それをふむやうな位置に私はゐた

晩年　*Ban'nen*

Someone

I came upon someone
She spoke to me
It was dark
I was at the center of something
A premonition of meeting someone subsided
And the someone quickly went away
It was an ordinary boring woman
The woman was trailing a long red cloth and
I was standing close enough to step on it

Twilight years (unpublished)

老いたるえびのうた

けふはえびのように悲しい
角(つの)やらひげやら
とげやら一杯生やしてゐるが
どれが悲しがつてゐるのか判らない。

ひげにたづねて見れば
おれではないといふ。
尖つたとげに聞いて見たら
わしでもないといふ。
それでは一体誰が悲しがつてゐるのか
誰に聞いてみても
さつぱり判らない。

生きてたたみを這うてゐるえせえび一疋。
からだじうが悲しいのだ。

遺作　[Isaku]

Song of an Old Prawn

Today I feel sad like a prawn
Even though I have feelers, whiskers
And lots of prickly bumps
I don't know which of them are feeling sad.

I ask the whisker
It says, Not me.
I ask the prickly bump
It says, Not me.
Who on earth, then, is feeling sad?
Whoever I ask
I get no answer.

A sham prawn lives, crawling on the tatami floor
Its entire body exudes sadness.

1962. [Posthumous]

KANEKO MITSUHARU
金子光晴

Kaneko Mitsuharu
(1895–1975)

LIFE AND CAREER

Kaneko Mitsuharu was a rebel all his life, combining uncommon insight into human nature with a fundamental distrust of conventions, traditions, and popular beliefs. His originality was evident right from his first unmistakably brilliant book of poems, which represented a radical departure from the mainstream. He conformed to no preconceived pattern. Though at heart he was an aesthete (he was also an accomplished painter), he did not isolate himself in a life of art, but remained engaged in the affairs of the world. He traveled widely in Europe and Asia, gaining an outsider's perspective on his own country. When Japan grew ultranationalistic under its oppressive military regime, he published antimilitary poems, which he continued to write in secret during the war. He remained a rebel in the postwar years as well, speaking out against Vietnam and other wars and vocally criticizing policies he opposed.

His complex personality was shaped by the unusual circumstances of his early life, recounted in his autobiography, *Poet*. At two years of age his bankrupt birth parents entrusted him to the care of a hairdresser. Kaneko was "fair-skinned and cuddly, and loved to draw pictures like a born painter." At the hairdresser's shop the sixteen-year-old wife of Kaneko Sōtarō, a wealthy construction company executive, "picked me up, and she did not put me down. ... She negotiated with my birth parents as if she were buying a doll, and officially adopted me. ... My adoptive mother was a girl, rather than a woman, petulant, self-centered, and extravagant; she was abnormally definitive about the distinctions between her likes and dislikes and what's beautiful and what's ugly. She treated me like a play doll, dressing me in girl's clothes, letting my hair grow so it could be shaped in a girly fashion. ... My playmates were all girls."[1] This extraordinary upbringing left an indelible mark on his precocious psyche, making him prematurely cynical, observant, and willful, traits that affected choices he made in later life and that contributed to the power of his poetry.

Kaneko's adoptive family moved to Kyoto in 1898, a year after his adoption, and he started elementary school there in 1901. Kyoto's combination of natural beauty and weighty tradition made a strong impression on the young boy. In 1905 the family moved to Tokyo, and Kaneko began to display the searching curiosity and insight into truth that persisted throughout his life. He was ten years old when he was attracted to Christianity and baptized in a local church. At the same time he started taking lessons in Japanese-style painting from a well-known *ukiyo-e*[2] artist, raising expectations of his becoming a great painter. One year later, having transferred to a new school, he lost interest in schoolwork. Beset by a vague unease and a longing to see America, he decided to run away with a friend. The two boys got only as far as the local seaport. At that point Kaneko had not yet finished primary school.

When Kaneko entered middle school at twelve, he placed high in his class in academic studies, and earned the school's top ranking in painting. Within a couple of years he was skipping school to frequent a local library and read Chinese classics. His voracious reading extended to the historical and popular novels of the Edo period[3] as well as books of Chinese philosophy and historical fiction. His devotion to this reading was obsessive, and he collected several thousand original

---

1. Kaneko, *Poet*, 17.

2. *Ukiyo-e* is the Japanese traditional art of both brush painting and woodblock printing, depicting the common customs and manners of the Edo period.

3. The Edo period (1603–1867) is the span of approximately 250 years of feudalism that preceded the Meiji Restoration. Edo was the political center of feudal Japan; its name became Tokyo when it was established as the country's capital after the Meiji Restoration.

editions of Edo literature.[4] He wrote some stories in the manner of popular Edo writers, but was not serious about writing.

Kaneko entered Waseda University in 1913 to major in English literature, but was soon disappointed with the department's emphasis on Naturalism, in reaction to which he flaunted his decadence and nihilism. By his own account he was so devoted to Oscar Wilde's *Salome* and *The Picture of Dorian Gray* and to Mikhail Artsybashev's *Sanin* that at nineteen he tried to emulate Dorian Gray and Sanin.[5] In 1915 he left Waseda University and enrolled first in the Japanese painting program at Tokyo Fine Arts College, then in Keio University's department of English literature. He was writing short stories and some haiku and *tanka*, but he did not discover modern poetry until 1916, when he was bedridden for three months with pneumonia. A friend encouraged him to read poetry, and he wrote some of his own. He also started reading modern French and English poetry and criticism. He was impressed with Arthur Symons's introduction to symbolism[6] and felt a kinship with Baudelaire.

His adoptive father died in 1917, leaving Kaneko a considerable inheritance, which he spent recklessly. But in 1918, when he read Walt Whitman's poem "To a Common Prostitute," Kaneko was moved by the idea of living with love and respect for all humanity. In that same year, Edward Carpenter's *Toward Democracy* led him to sympathize with democratic ideals. These new discoveries caused him to "shed Wilde as if stepping out of my underwear,"[7] and his searching eye turned to reality and truths in life's phenomena.

In 1919 Kaneko self-published *Akatsuchi no ie* (House of red clay), which received hardly any notice, and left for London with an antiques dealer, a family friend, who hoped to groom Kaneko to become an international antiques dealer. But as Kaneko did not show any inclina-

---

4. Kaneko, *Poet*, 42.
5. Ibid., 59.
6. Arthur Symons (1865–1945) was a British poet, critic, and translator. "His seminal guide *The Symbolist Movement in Literature* (1899) introduced English readers to the Symbolist movement, which Symons described as 'an attempt to spiritualize literature'." https://www.poetryfoundation.org/poets/arthur-symons.
7. Kaneko, *Poet*, 81.

tion for the business, the dealer arranged for Kaneko to stay comfortably in Brussels, Belgium, for a full year. There Kaneko devoted his time to reading contemporary European poetry, notably over twenty volumes of Emile Verhaeren's poetry, which taught him "the secret of expressions that come alive"[8] as he overlaid the scenery around him with lines from Verhaeren's poems. He also filled many notebooks with his own poems. He extended his trip, staying in Paris for several more months, and returned home in 1921.

Upon his return to Japan the poems he had written in Belgium caught the attention of his circle of young poets as "exceptional poetry, which no one in Japan has ever attempted."[9] This recognition led to the publication of his *Koganemushi* (Gold beetle) in 1923. His own preface prepares the reader for colorful hallucinatory dreams and recollections, with reference to Baudelaire's "Le Voyage,"[10] in the pursuit of decadent beauty and of truth in humanity. But his books of poetry did not sell, and he had lost his inheritance in speculative business ventures, which left him in desperate financial straits. He married Mori Michiyo, an aspiring novelist, in 1924 with the poet Murō Saisei's blessing, and in 1925 they had a son. In 1928, leaving their son with his wife's parents, and temporarily abandoning his literary ambitions, he and his wife left for Southeast Asia. They traveled from the coastal cities of China to Java and Malaya. He held exhibits of his paintings in cities along the way to earn money for survival. In 1930 they settled in Paris, struggling to survive for two years, "taking any conceivable job for food, with no time to read or write." Living among the citizens of Paris, and travelling through Southeast Asian countries on his way home, he was exposed to disapproval of Japan's military policy and

---

8. Ibid., 94.
9. Ibid., 102.
10. "Le Voyage" is the concluding poem of Baudelaire's poetic masterpiece, *Les fleurs du mal (Flowers of evil)*. "The 1861 edition consists of 126 poems arranged in six sections of varying length. ... The collection may best be read in the light of the concluding poem, *Le Voyage,* as a journey through self and society in search of some impossible satisfaction that forever eludes the traveler." See https://www.britannica.com/biography/Charles-Baudelaire#ref149676

developed more objective views of the current state of affairs with regard to his native country.

When the couple returned to Japan in 1932, Kaneko felt alienated in his homeland, among apathetic fellow citizens and even his old friends, in the face of loud ultranationalistic propaganda. Determined to be truthful to his own convictions, he wrote and published poems opposing Japan's war effort, such as "The Lighthouse" in 1935, which younger poets assumed was written by "a young poet of twenty-something, although I was forty,"[11] as Kaneko recalled. He was critical of the magazines *Shiki* (Four seasons) and *Rekitei* (Journey), which were powerful and influential at the time, because he felt that the poets who published in these magazines tended to be "too intent on making a well-composed masterpiece, by refining their technique." Instead he resolved "to examine the circumstances surrounding poetry, to pursue the truth, and to write only what I wanted to write."[12] With this resolve, and with his desire to get around the increasingly strict censorship of the military regime, he carefully constructed rich verbiage in which he symbolically sculpted his truth. Kaneko wrote poems, "obfuscating some lines, … almost in collusion with the editor"[13] to sneak them past the censors, but many of his poems were rejected. In 1937 he published a book of antiwar and resistance poems *Same* (Sharks). Even after he lost all outlets for his work, Kaneko continued writing poems attacking or ridiculing the fundamental premise of Japan's imperialism and colonialism in an environment where such subversive poetry, if discovered, could have cost him his life.

In 1943, with air raids intensifying, he and his family moved from Tokyo to a cottage on the lake in the foothills of Mount Fuji. As Itō Shinkichi points out, moving away from Tokyo was not just a prudent measure by which Kaneko could secure his safety, but an act of protest as well. It meant "nothing but becoming an exile … and his poetry was his last will and testament. Kaneko Mitsuharu wrote his poetry in

---

11. Kaneko, *Poet*, 185.
12. Ibid.
13. Kaneko, *Zenshishū*, 639.

hiding, and buried it under the frozen water of the lake. If it had been discovered, what would have happened to him? Each poem expressed his furious anger against the war."[14]

A year after the war ended he settled back in Tokyo with his family, and set out to publish three books containing the subversive poems he wrote during the war years. *Rakkasan* (Parachute), published in 1948, collected poems written "after Japan started its war with China [in 1937] and until ten days or so before the end of World War II. All were written purposefully for publication, and almost half of them were published under difficult and risky circumstances."[15] *Ga* (Moths) contained "poems written after air raids became quite frequent and up until a week before the end of the war, ... because I was tormented by despair and lamenting over the crazed foolhardiness of the endlessly continuing war."[16] And in 1949 he published *Oni no ko no uta* (Songs of the ogre's children), which contained poems written from around the time the Sino-Japanese war started in 1937 through May of 1945. A few had been published during the war, some were submitted to and rejected by publishers, but the majority were written with no hope of publication.[17] After these three volumes, he moved on to his postwar work, and published seven books of poetry as well as several prose works of his observations and philosophical essays on human nature and the Japanese people, along with assembling and editing the authorized edition of his collected poetry. He closely observed his fellow Japanese while desperately trying to survive in a chaotic and deprived postwar Tokyo in order to gain insight into the nature of man.

Ningen no higeki (Tragedy of man), containing poems written during the years after the war, was published in 1952, and awarded the fifth Yomiuri Literary Prize in 1953.[18] The poems in this collection are generally long and often combined with prose soliloquys, and are col-

---

14. Itō Shinkichi, *Shi no furusato* (Birthplaces of poems) (Tokyo: Shinchōsha, 1974), 119.
15. Kaneko, *Zenshishū*, 639.
16. Ibid., 488.
17. Ibid., 545.
18. *Yomiuri Bungaku shō*, established in 1949 by the Yomiuri Newspaper Company for the purpose of helping to restore literary activities.

ored with a deep and depressive view of humanity and existence. His last book of poems, *IL* (1965), was awarded the Rekitei Prize in 1966. This book contains poems, prose poems, and hybrids of the two forms, in which the poet examines his inner truth from the vantage point of seventy years of existence. These poems are too long to include here in their entirety, and unfortunately excerpts do not do them justice.

Kaneko also published several Japanese translations of European poetry, such as *Selected Poems of [Emile] Verhaeren* and *Kindai Furansu Shishu* (Anthology of French poetry) (both 1925), *Selected Poems of [Arthur] Rimbaud* (1951), *Selected Poems of [Louis] Aragon* (1951), and *Baudelaire: Les Fleurs du Mal* (1952). He passed away in 1975.

POETRY

Throughout his career Kaneko exhibited a powerfully creative imagination, a discerning eye for beauty, and unflinching attention to realities and truths hidden beneath the surface of human affairs. The clarity and objectivity of his vision and world view were no doubt developed in part from his experiences during his extensive travels abroad. But the Western viewpoints he absorbed while living in Europe were often in conflict with the inherently Japanese cultural conditioning of his inner being once he was back in Japan. He was a complex and conflicted genius, whose rich reservoir of linguistic and literary knowledge, acquired through years of voracious reading in Asian and Western literatures, enhanced by his painter's eye, gave him a distinct and captivating poetic voice with which he chose to be decadent, despairing, detached, cutting, cynical, or resigned, depending on his subject matter and his creative viewpoint.

In his first book, *Koganemushi* (Gold beetle), his lines generate the impression of an elaborate tapestry decorated in iridescent colors. The figures of the tapestry move in a carefully measured listless rhythm, as evident in the title poem. While this kind of texture is difficult to capture in translation, its content is solidly transferrable, with the dreamlike recollections of inexplicable experiences from boyhood looming as powerful and enigmatic presences.

In the second book, *Mizu no rurō* (Vagrant water), which collects poems and prose poems he wrote over the "five, six years after [the poems in] *Koganemushi*,"[19] his style is very different. "Seagulls" still carries some rich and ornate images, but "Used Shoe Shop," for example, is a narrative casually told by a customer haunted by the sad social reality lurking behind the used shoes on display in a shabby store. Kaneko's empathy with the downtrodden and dejected is a strong undercurrent in much of his poetry, although he is neither sentimental nor emotional about it. The voice can be smooth and cool in one case, vulgar in another, cutting, cynical, or ironical in yet another. Kaneko's expert use of different manners of speech according to gender, age, social status, or cultural taste quickly generates an atmosphere in which the reader shares the experience with the voice of the poem.

In his subversive antiwar, anti-Imperialist poetry the poet's voice, both cynical and intense, is supported by startling images. "The Lighthouse" was published in *Same* (Sharks) in 1937, when the divine and absolute authority of the Emperor was daily drilled into the Japanese people's psyche. Within this context the poem is a daring rejection of the whole premise of the then-current belief system, wrapped in a masterfully surrealistic presentation of fantastic images.

"Angels," expressing "repudiation of the draft and war-weariness,"[20] was written about a week before the war ended, "when my mind was feeling weak, helpless because of despair and sorrow over the crazed stupidity of a war with no end in sight."[21] It was included in *Rakkasan* (Parachute), published in 1948. In its postscript he writes, "At a glance the poetry here may seem to have completed its mission, but I believe that is not yet the case at all. The distress in this poetry may be relevant to us in the future. I will first publish a few collections of poems written during the war, and then I would like to move on."[22]

---

19. Kaneko, *Zenshishū*, 875.
20. Kaneko, *Poet*, 189.
21. Kaneko, *Zenshishū*, 195.
22. Ibid., 639.

He did move on, actively involving himself in literary activities such as becoming a founding member of a poetry magazine *Ainame* (Rock trout) in 1964, publishing five more books of poetry, books of autobiography and autobiographical essays, and three books of critical essays on the Japanese people and Japanese art. But he never seemed to find peace with himself or with the world he lived in. In his books of poems, such as 1955's *Hijō* (Heartless), the tone of his voice is negative and cynical. Perhaps it reflects his disappointment in the world that came into being after the end of a war that he risked his life to oppose. His genius was restless and brilliant to the end.

金亀子（こがねむし）

柳蔭暗く、煙咽鳴する頃、
黄丁字の花、幽かにこぼれ敷く頃、
新月（にひづき）、繊（ほそ）くのぼる頃

常夜燈を廻る金亀子の如く
少年は、戀慕し、嘆く。

　　　　二

其夜、少年は秘符の如く、美しい巴旦杏の少女を胸にいだく。
少年の焔の頬は櫻桃（ゆすらうめ）の如くうららかであった。
少年のはぢらひの息は紅貝の如くかがようた。

おづおづと寄り添ふおそれに慄へつつ
少年の悲しいまごころは、
花朧（はなおぼろ）が如く危惧を夢みてゐた。

煩悩焦思の梢、梢を、
鶏冠菜（とさかのり）の如くかき乱れた。

少年は身も魂も破船の如くうちくだけた。
ああ、盲目の蘆蒼や焚香にむせびつつ、
少年は嗤ふべき見せ物であった。
　　　　　　　（戀の風流こそ優しけれ
　　　　　　　　戀の堕獄こそ愛（めで）たけれ）

金亀子　*Koganemushi*

Gold Beetle

When smoke sobs, in the dark shade of willows
When yellow clove flowers spill quietly to pave over the walk
When the new moon rises thin

The boy yearns in love, moaning,
Like a gold beetle circling a night lamp.

II

That night, the boy held a lovely almond girl close to his chest, like a
    secret charm
His flaming cheeks were as bright as cherries
His bashful breaths glowed like crimson shellfish.

Timidly snuggling close trembling with awe
His pitiful devotion
Conjured apprehension like a prickly pink fish.

He was frenetic swaying like crimson seaweeds
Between peaks of lust and anxiety.

The boy was a shipwreck, crushed to pieces, body and soul.
Ah, blinded, suffocated in aloe and burning incense,
He was a circus clown.
        (Tender is love's grace
        Lovable is love's damnation)

1923. *Gold beetle*

海の小品

　　一　鷗

　　神代ながらの火の岩鼻に、
むらがり聚ってふぢ壺が、地のうなり、天のとどろきをきく。
紫の岩洞奥ふかく飛沫(しぶき)は、鬣(たてがみ)ふつてをどり込む。
清澄な朝の全海景ほ、潮煙りに送られる。

そのとき岩礁に影をおとし、
天使たちが提げる金の聖龕燈、
二羽の鷗が、蒼冥を横ぎつてゆく。
プラチナの燈臺さして、
いのちの細笛をふきつれて。

　　二　燈臺にて

沖へ。鱗族(いろくず)どもが背をすり合せ、のり越え、競ふ大洋へ。
瞬間にいのちを賭けて、沖へ、沖へ、わたしは若い。

わしはかへつてきた。あそこから、闘ひに疲れ、憩ひをもとめ、
入江に抱かれ、松籟の渚に巻き返し、身をまろばせて眠るため。

白晝、燈臺下の焼岩から両足をたらし、目をとぢて、
私は、うづ巻く波濤のざわめきのなかに、この二つの言葉をきい
　　た。

水の流浪　*Mizu no rurō*

Short Pieces on the Sea

    I   Seagulls

At the nose of the fiery rock just as it was in the age of gods,
barnacles crowd together and hear the earth groan, the heavens roar.
sprays of water, waving their manes, burst into the deep of the
    purple rock cave.
the tidal mist sees off the entire seascape of the pure and clear
    morning.

In that moment, casting shadows on the reef,
angels carry holy golden lanterns,
two seagulls fly across the emerald world.
heading for a platinum lighthouse,
blowing life's piccolo along the way.

    II   At the Lighthouse

"Head out to the open sea! To the great ocean where scaly tribes rub
    against, ride over, and race with one another!
I head out to the open sea, to the open sea, betting my life on the
    moment. I am young."

"I am back. From there, tired of battles, seeking peaceful rest, so that
I sleep, lulled on the shore by the breeze through the pines, embraced
    by the arm of the sea."

Mid-day, dangling my legs from the sunbaked rock by the lighthouse,
    I closed my eyes and
I heard these two voices in the agitation of swirling surges.

1926. *Vagrant water*

古靴店

　いまにもふりだしさうな五月空(さつきぞら)。
うらぶれた港町の、一軒の古靴店。

軒につるした古靴はどれもこれも
踵がちび、革が破れ、いづれ修繕しつくして、なほしがきかない廃
　　れもの。
いまの落魄が、一入身に沁みる華著型や、
時代おくれなふかゴムや、

色紙だらけの學生靴。
權勢の俤失せぬ長靴や、子供靴、
それぞれに、どんな海路をわたりつかれて、
あつまつてきたぼろ舟たちか。

おお、かなしくも諷諭的なこのながめよ。

私は猶も、そのなかから、足にあふ伴侶を物色する。

知ってるよ。どこかの人の汗や足脂でぎちぎちになった底革や、突
　　き出た釘の痛さなど。

知ってるよ。しみこんでくる水のつめたさや、泣きたさや、
おちぶれたものの心にかよひあふ、私たち同士のほろりとしたお
　　もひやりふかい言葉など。

水の流浪　*Mizu no rurō*

Used Shoe Shop

The May sky is threatening rain now.
a used-shoe shop, in a seedy port town.

every and each pair of used shoes hung under the eave
is junk: heels worn, leather torn, repaired to death.
an elegant pair whose currently reduced circumstances hits me hard,
a pair of long rubber boots of yesteryear,

a pair of student's shoes with colored paper all over.
a pair of tall boots still carrying an air of authority, and kids' shoes,
how did each cross the sea, exhausted,
to come together, these rickety boats?

oh, this sad and redolent sight!

I still hunt among them for a companion for my feet.

I know, y'know. The pain from a leather sole shrunk by the sweat and
 grease of someone else's foot, with tacks sticking through it.

I know, y'know. How cold water is when it leaks, how I feel
 like crying,
and how caring words connect our hearts, among us, the down-
 trodden.

1926. *Vagrant water*

上水にて

きれいに澄んだ秋空に、
石橋の二本の親柱(おやばしら)が、
立ってゐた。二人の
白服をきた巡査(おまわりさん)のやうに。

砲口掃除の大ブラッシのやうな穂を
八方に突出したかもじぐさの縦列、
ながれの塘のきなくさい青空のなかを、折釘ほどの小ささで、
俺の姿が、散歩する。

すばやい風が、桐林を裏返す。枝にかかった結婚指環を鳴らし、
ふはついた俺の髪をなぶり、ながれのわらしべを、ゆく雲を見送
　る。

ああ。このきれいで、あとくされない、澄んだ風よ。
俺の心から、ちぎってすててくれ。借財などでくよくよする根性を。
小鳥も、木の葉もちりぢりになって、
この俺のあたまからふってくる。

手にした「古詩箋註」をひろげ、しかし、よまないで
俺はあるく。
すばやい風が、コスモスの白を、蓼の紅を、ひきむしり、
俺の思想にはなしるをかける。

きれいに澄んだ秋空。
次の橋の親柱で、またも
立ってゐる。二人の
白服をきた巡査。

水の流浪　　*Mizu no rurō*

On the Reservoir

Against the completely clear autumn sky
the two main support pillars of the stone bridge
stand. Like two
policemen in white uniforms.

The column of a platoon of wheat grass stands with ears sticking out
    in all directions
like large brushes for cleaning the muzzles of guns,
in the disquieting blue sky at the bank of an inlet, as small as a bent nail,
my figure, takes a walk.

Quick winds flip the grove of paulownias, clink the wedding bands
    hung on the branches,
toy with my unkempt hair, send off the hay flowing away; clouds pass on.

Ah! you, the beautiful clear wind with no concern for future troubles!
tear away from my petty heart worrying over debts and such trifles!
small birds and tree leaves all scatter,
to rain down from my head.

I open the book of Annotated Classic Poetry, but instead of reading it
I walk.
a quick wind, tearing away the white of cosmos and the crimson of
    knot grass,
sprays nose drippings over my thoughts.

The completely clear autumn sky.
at the main support pillars of the next bridge, again
stand two
policemen in white uniforms.

1926. *Vagrant water*

寒山寺

瓦路、雑草のしげみがふかい。
若楡のかぼそい樹林の蔭、疎らに、
石にはすべて白苔がむし、甍はまるで雀や鵝で囀り立ててゐるや
　　うな、
さびはてた吊鐘、陶製のみどりの窓桟。
白壁の廻廊も大頹破し
後庭は廃れて
白蝶の群るのみ。

寒山寺は寂々として、陽は物淋しい。
夏日は、楓橋を燕がくぐり
秋は果(このみ)、響高く割れ、草の穂は影とちり
冬はとりわけ碑石の膚冷たく
寒林がただ凍れる雲を突刺す

鱶沈む　*Fuka shizumu*

KANZANJI TEMPLE

A tiled walk, the thick growth of weeds.
Shade in the grove of scrawny young elms, sparse,
The stones are all thick with white moss,
The roof tiles seem to scream with sparrows and finches,
The rusted-out dome-shaped bell, the green ceramic window sills.
The white walls along the corridors have fallen down
The back yard is desolate
But for swarming white butterflies.

Kanzanji is in isolation, and the sunlight is forlorn.
On a summer's day swallows sweep through a tunnel of maples
In autumn, nuts loudly crack, and ears of grass are blown away into
    shadows
In winter, the tombstones are particularly cold to the touch
Only the frosty trees skewer frozen clouds

1927. *Sharks sink*

ペダンの夜

　ペダンの夜。
大気は女の肉香で息苦しい。
遠く、ものがなしい笛が、毒蛇を誘(おび)いてゐる

炎暑でつらいからだを、腹這ひになって、
女は、ごろごろ鳴る腹を、石でひやしてゐた。
……そのひらべったい腰のまはりを飾らうとおもつて
私は、じぶんの前歯をコンコン砕(か)いてゐた。

驟雨(シャワー)！！！
ふたりがはじめて抱きあって泣いた芳舎を
熱水の雨の瀧つ瀬が、破れた蕃扇のやうにゆすぶった
(おおその女は、夜、夜は今どこにある。)

その晩雨水をふるふ森のなかを
雨晴れのすずしい風がふきぬけた。
黒い野猿(やえん)がキ、キと叫ぶ枝のしたを、
鮠魚(はや)を突く土蕃のまる木舟がおりた。

ぴんらう椰子のならぶ海岸には
南の星座が、繊形花をひらいた。

路傍の愛人　*Robō no aijin*

Night in Pedang

Night in Pedang.
The air is stuffy with the scent of women's flesh.
A distant, sorrowful flute seduces a poisonous snake

Fatigued in burning heat, lying flat on her belly,
the woman was cooling her growling stomach with a stone
… I was noisily chipping my own front teeth
hoping to adorn her flat rear end.

A shower!!!
waterfalls of heated rain shook the fragrant shack
where the two of us first embraced and cried, like a torn grass-fan
(oh, where is the woman, the night, where is that night now?)

After the rain that night cool breezes
passed through the forest shaking down raindrops.
Under the branches where black monkeys squealed
a dugout went down the river carrying a native spear-fishing dace.

Over the shore lined with areca palms
The southern constellation opened an umbrella of flowers.

1928. *Lovers on the roadside*

燈臺

　　　　一

そらのふかさをのぞいてはいけない。
そらのふかさには、
神さまたちがめじろおししてゐる。

飴のやうなエーテルにただよふ、
天使の腋毛。
鷹のぬけ毛。

青銅(からかね)の灼けるやうな凄じい神さまたちのはだのにほひ。
　　秤(かんかん)。

そらのふかさをみつめてはいけない。
その眼はひかりでやきつぶされる。

そらのふかさからおりてくるものは、永劫にわたる権力だ。

そらにさからふものへの
刑罰だ。

信心ふかいたましひだけがのぼる。
そらのまんなかにつつたつた、
いつぼんのしろい蝋燭。
　　——燈臺。

　　　　二

それこそは天の燈守(あかしもり)。海のみちしるべ
　　(こゝろのまづしいものは、福(さいはひ)なるかな)
包茎。
禿頭のソクラテス。

The Lighthouse

I

Do not peer into the depths of the sky.
The depths of the sky
Are crowded with gods.

An angel's underarm hair
A falcon's molt
Drift in caramelized ether.

Fierce smell of gods' skin, like burning bronze. A blazing balance.

Do not stare at the depths of the sky.
Its light will burn your eyes to blindness.

Descending from the depths of the sky is the eternal power.

That is the punishment
For those who defy the sky.

Only a devout soul can ascend.
A single white candle
Stands tall in the middle of the sky.
—the lighthouse.

II

It is the light-keeper of heaven. The ocean's guidepost
    (Blessed are the poor in spirit)
Phimosis.
Baldheaded Socrates.

薔薇の花のにほひを焚きこめる朝暾の、燈臺の白堊にそうて、辿りながら、おいらはそのまはりを一巡りする。めやにだらけなこの眼が、はるばるといただきをながめる。

神......三位一體。愛。不滅の眞理。それら至上のことばの苗床。ながれる瑠璃のなかの、一滴の乳。

神さまたちの咳や、いきざれが手にとるやうにきこえるふかさで、燈臺はただよひ、

燈臺は、耳のやうにそよぐ。

　　　　三

こころをうつす明鏡だといふそらをかつては、忌みおそれ、
——神はゐない。
と、おろかにも放言した。
それだのにいまこの身邊の、神のいましめのきびしいことはどうだ。うまれおちるといふことは、まづ、このからだを神にうられたことだった。おいらたちのいのちは、神の富であり、犧とならば、すすみたつてこのいのちをすてねばならないのだ。
・・・・・・・・・・・。
・・・・・・・・・・・。

つぶて、翼、唾、弾丸（たま）、なにもとどかぬたかみで、安閑として、
神は下界をみおろしてゐる。
かなしみ、憎み、天のくらやみを指して、おいらは叫んだ。
——それだ。そいつだ。そいつを曳きずりおろすんだ。

In the heavenly sunrise infused with the scent of roses,
I make a full circle of the lighthouse, sliding along its limestone wall.
My mucus-filled eyes look up far at its top.

God … Trinity. Love. Eternal Truth. The nursery of these supreme
    words. A drop of milk in the fluid lapis lazuli.

In the depths where the gods' coughing and panting are heard close
    by
the lighthouse drifts,

the lighthouse sways like an ear.

III

Once I feared and loathed the sky said to be the clear mirror that
    reflects my heart
and foolishly declared,
—"There is no God."
But how about this tight constraint of God? Birth was, first of all, a
    sale of my body to God. My life is God's wealth, and I must offer
    my life, if sacrifice is needed.
. . . .
. . . .

God looks down over our world
in peaceful leisure, from a height where stones, wings, spit, bullets or
    whatever could never reach.
I screamed pointing at sorrows, hatred, and heaven's darkness.
—"Yes! That's Him. Drag Him down."

だが、おいらたち、おもひあがった神の冒瀆者、自由を求めるもの
　　のうへに、たちまち、冥罰はくだつた。
雷鳴。
いや、いや、それは、
燈臺の鼻つ先でぶんぶんまはる
ひつつこい蠅ども。
威嚇するやうに雁行し、
つめたい歯をむきだしてひるがへる

一つ
一つ
神託をのせた
五臺の水上爆撃機。

鮫　*Same*

But God's stealthy punishment swiftly descended upon us, conceited
    and profane seekers of freedom.
Thunder.
No, no. They are,
persistent flies
buzzing around right at the tip of the lighthouse.
In a wild-geese formation, threatening
flipping over, bearing cold teeth

one
by one
carrying divine revelation
five carrier-based bombers.

1937. *Sharks*

洗面器

（僕は長年のあひだ、洗面器といふうつはは、僕たちが顔や手を洗ふのに湯、水を入れるものとばかり思つてゐた。ところが爪哇(ジャワ)人たちはそれに羊(カンピン)や魚(イカン)や、鶏や果実などを煮込んだカレー汁をなみなみとたたへて、花咲く合歓木(ねむ)の木陰でお客を待つてゐるし、その同じ洗面器にまたがって広東(カントン)の女たちは、嫖客(へうかく)の目の前で不浄をきよめしやぼりしやぼりとさびしい音をたてて尿(いばり)をする。）

　洗面器のなかの
さびしい音よ。

くれてゆく岬(タンジョン)の
雨の碇泊(とまり)。

ゆれて、
傾いて、
疲れたこころに
いつまでもはなれぬひびきよ。

人の生のつづくかぎり。
耳よ。おぬしは聴くべし。

洗面器のなかの
音のさびしさを。

女たちへのエレジー　*On'na tachi e no elegy*

Washbasin

(For many years I have thought that a washbasin is for water to wash face and hands. But the Javanese use it to cook sheep, fish, fowl and fruits in abundant curry sauce, and wait for customers in the shade of flowering silk trees. The same washbasin—women in Guangdong cleanse their impurity and urinate into it, splashing a sad sound, in front of the guests at a brothel.)

Sad sound,
In the washbasin.

In a lodge in rain
At the headland as the night falls.

In my rippling
Pitching and
Tired heart
The sound lingers with no end.

As long as humans have life.
You, ears, you must listen to it.

The sadness of the sound
Into washbasins.

1949. *An elegy for women*

あけがたの歌　序詩

　　　　一

　　燈(あかり)を消さう。そのうちもうあけがただよ。
水腫(すゐしゆ)のあま皮をはがす剃刀(かみそり)のやうな
鋭利なあさあけ。
ひらかれた窓からながれいる
爽やかな悲愁。

　　紙幣。このひとときには、それも、うすぼけた紙きれとしかみえない。
　　窓外の風景は、しらけきって、ねざめぎはの夢のあとをおって
　　どっかへ逃れてゆかうとさまよふ。
　　僕も、僕のつれあるいてゐる影も、ゆくところがない。

地平線、

そのうへに重なる灰色の屍(しかばね)。
るいるいとしたからだ。

大河の氾濫につづく洪水。
そのうへをわたって
細いマッチ棒のやうな錐柱(すゐちゆう)。
ならぶ百本の煙突。

遠い海峡の潮の音。

かへらないためにとびたつ
戦闘機。

Song of Dawn: A Prefatory Poem

I

Put out the light. It'll soon be dawn.
Sharp-edged daybreak
Like a blade to peel away the epidermis from an edema.
Refreshing sorrows
Flow in from the open window.

> Paper money. This moment it just looks like an old piece of paper.
> The scenery from the window is pallid, chasing the dream at waking,
> Drifting to seek a place for escape.
> Neither I nor my companion, my shadow, have a destination.

Horizon,

On which ashen corpses pile.
Bodies heaped up.

Great River overflows and floods.
Crossing over it
Are tapered pillars like slender matchsticks.
A hundred chimneys lined up.

The tidal roar of the distant strait.

Fighter planes take off
Never meant to return.

　　　　二

　　ががぶたや、水かまきりや、あたまもしつぼもづんぐりしためくら
　　　魚どもが
泥沼のなかを横行してゐる。
陰謀と、うそと、醜(みにく)さが、こんなにはっきりみえてることはない。
出発しよう。さあ。
まだ誰も起きてない街をそつと通りぬけて、

敷石のしたからきこえてくる
亡びたジャズの雨音。

うなされてゐる画ビラ。

涙にしめつたコンクリと、
汗をかいた銃。

あのながい塀のうちは
屈従、
屈従、
屈従、
どんな恥も
屈従よりはいくらかましだ。

いなづま。
いや、さうぢやないよ。あれは、
誰かが白鶴となって朝空に舞上るため
じぶんの頭に、たまをうちこんだのだ。

　　　　　　　　　　　　　　昭和十九・八・七

落下傘　*Rakkasan*

II

Water weeds, water scorpions, stumpy blind fish
Move about in the swamp.
Intrigues, lies, and ugliness have never been so clearly visible.
Let us start out. Now.
Stealthily passing through the streets where no one else is awake yet,

From under the paved stones
Comes the extinct jazz sound of rain.

An illustrated flyer groaning in bad dreams.

Cement soaked with tears and
A sweating gun.

Inside that long wall is
Submission
Submission
Submission
Whatever the shame is
It is better than submission.

Lightning!
No, that's not it. That's ...
Someone, wanting to turn into a white crane to soar into the
    morning sky,
Just shot a bullet into his own head.

(Aug 7, 1944)

1948. *Parachute*

天使

　　　一

　しやぼん玉があがるやうに
嬰児(あかんぼ)たちが
そらにうかぶ。

神の煉乳(コンデンス・ミルク)で育つた
薔薇の膚(はだ)は
風邪をひかない。
むつきもいらない。

その背には
雉鳩(きじばと)のつばさ。

花の輪のやうに手を繋ぎ、
雲や手巾(ハンカチーフ)のやうに
夕ぞらにただよふ

おお。天使(エンゼル)よ。

きらきらと
貝殻鏤(ちりば)めた天のおくに
天使らはむらがり遊ぶといふ。

天使らの純真な笑ひ声が
あそこにみちあふれるといふ。

　　　二

　だが、いま、嬰児たちは顔蒼(あを)褪め
アビオグラムのなかを遁(のが)れまはる。

Angels

I

Just like soap bubbles floating up
Babies
Float in the sky.

Their rosy skin is
Nurtured with God's condensed milk.
They do not catch cold.
They need no diapers.

They sport turtle doves' wings
On their backs.

Hand in hand like a ring of flowers
They drift in the evening sky
Like clouds and handkerchiefs

Oh, Angels!

Angels flock and play, they say,
In the depths of heavens inlaid with shells
Glittering

Angels' innocent laughter, they say,
Brims over there.

II

But now the babies' faces are white
Inside a radar map, trying to find a way out.

成層圏まで、父なる主宰者はゐまさず
嬰児たちは孤児となりはてた。
塵や、木の葉や、新聞紙とともに、かれらは
宙に吹きちらされる。

口いっぱい蟹の泡を噴き
うろたへ、
逆さになり、くるくる廻り、
べたべたなキャンディを手で握り、
肉桂(にくけい)のにほふ甘つたるいからだ、
すつぱい林檎(りんご)。
円光(リング)を背負った
無心な天使らは
地球にやすらふところがない。

踏んづけるほどおっぱいが押しあつても
天使らを養ふものはゐない。
気球のあがる
屋上のたたきのうへで、
飴いろのにぎやかな一群を
秋空たかく、私は
かなしげに見送る。

あはれ、邪(よこしま)と
疑(うたがひ)をしらぬもの、
えらばれた扈従(こしょう)たちよ。
いづくにゆく。

　昼の月、
浮雲とともに
神の声色(こわいろ)、遠雷のつぶやく
くにざかひのそらを天使らは
おそれげもなく
膝(ひざ)で
匍(は)ひまはる。

落下傘　*Rakkasan*

The presiding august Father is not present even in the stratosphere.
The babies have become orphans.
They are blown about in the air
Along with dust, tree leaves, and newsprint.

Spewing mouthfuls of crab bubbles
Frenetic,
Upside down, circling,
Clasping sticky candies in their hands,
Their sweet flesh smelling of cinnamon,
Acidic apples.
Innocent angels
Sporting halos
Have no place to rest on Earth.

Even where breasts are so numerous and pressed together
None will nurse angels.
Standing on the bare concrete rooftop
Where hot balloons take off,
I sadly see off
The amber-colored lively flock
High into the autumn sky.

Poor you, chosen servants
Ignorant of evil
And doubt,
Where are you heading?

   In the sky above the nation's border
Where distant thunder, God's voice, growls
Along with the moon in mid-day
And floating clouds
Angels fearlessly
Crawl about
On their knees.

1948. *Parachute*

卵の唄

　　——大地獄、小地獄のふつふつとたぎる泥のなかで、鬼は卵を孵(かへ)す。卵は猶火焔に抱かれてねむる。鳴動する岩、ちぎれとぶ雲。

　　三本の指をたたんだ
皺だらけな蹠(あしうら)は
うへむきにひらく。
宇宙が秤(はか)る
「我」のおもたさ。

法官たちは
ならんで見護る。
この鬼怪(きくわい)の芽が
殻のなかで
宇宙を夢みるのを。

相剋(さうこく)も、懊悩(あうなう)も、
悲運も、呪咀も
まだ天と地のやうに
はっきりとわかれず、
愛憎も混沌。

透(す)いた血の
鼈甲(べっかふ)いろのなかに
かたちの影がうごき
まづしのび入る
哀愁。

A Song of the Egg

—In the boiling mud of the Greater and Lesser Hells, Ogres incubate their eggs. The eggs are still asleep, held in flames. Rocks shake and roar. Clouds are torn and blown.

The wrinkled sole
With three toes folded in
Opens upward.
The universe measures
The weight of "Self."

Sitting side by side
Judges keep watch.
This monstrous offspring
Dreams of the universe
Inside the eggshell.

Conflicts, agony
Misfortune, and curses
Have not yet clearly separated
Like heaven and earth
Neither are Love and Hate in chaos.

Inside the amber color
Of limpid serum
A shadowy shape moves
And now pathos
Sneaks in.

痣(あざ)の毒と
氷塊のみどりから生れる
乳色のオパールの
ちらばる火が
いのちをみちびく。

火焔はなめる。
ながい舌で
みじかい舌で。
繻子(しゅす)のやうに包む。
悩みのかたまりを。

七殺の凶運を。
不可解な
智慧の篆文(てんぶん)を。
欲望のひこばえ、
禍(わざわひ)の端緒を。

鬼の児の歌　*Oni no ko no uta*

Life is guided
By fire sputtering
In milky opalescence
Born out of the birthmark's venom and
The iceberg's green.

Flames lick.
With stretched tongues
With stubby tongues.
They wrap like satin.
Lumps of anguish.

Seven murderous misfortunes.
Inscrutable
Ancient writings of wisdom.
Sprouts of desire,
Triggers of calamities.

1949. *Songs of the ogre's children*

鬼と詩人

詩人はみた。地獄の火を浴びて、天に立つ柱を。或は、吹雪のそら
　　に舞上るながい髭を。

詩人はみた、雲ゆきはやい空に、鬼どもの伸びあがる影を。
しやがんだ影を。

詩人の眼だけにみえるんだ。鼻の孔から出たり入ったりする小鬼。
紙幣をかぞへる鬼。女のすきな鬼。
だが、そんなやつは、どれもこれも、鼻汁をひっかけるにも足りぬ。

大鍋のなかの月を鐵の火箸ではさみあげる、諷刺畫めいた鬼ど
　　も。
そいつらも、
おもはせぶりだけで、あきあきものだ。

　　僕らが待ってゐるやつは、たつたいま、
熔鉱爐から裸でをどり出した、芥子粒のやうな鬼どもで、
やつらは自分でも、なにがなにやらわからない。
さはつたらやけどだ。ひぶくれだ。
僕らもやつらといっしょにとび廻る。さけび廻る。
詩をつくれ！　火をつけろ！

鬼の児の歌　　*Oni no ko no uta*

Ogres and Poet

Poet saw it: the pillar standing in heaven, bathed by Hell's flames; or a long beard flying up into the snowstorming sky.

Poet saw the shadows of ogres stretch up into the sky with the speeding clouds;
Their squatting shadows.

Only Poet's eyes can see them, y'know, those small ogres moving in and out of nostrils.
Money-counting ogres, womanizing ogres.
But they don't deserve a shower of nose drips.

Cartoon ogres lift the moon out of a gigantic pot with iron chopsticks.
They too are
Mere tantalizers. They bore me stiff.

We are waiting for
Ogres as small as poppy seeds, now dancing out of the blast furnace, naked.
They themselves don't know what is what.
If you touch them you'll be burnt, get blisters.
We romp around with them, scream with them.
Make poetry! Set fires!

1949. *Songs of the ogre's children*

昇天

けふは、非戦論者の処刑日だ。
銃声とともに倒れる屍(しかばね)からのがれて、
たましひは天へあがった。
不正不義を告げるため。

鬼どももかなしんでとけはじめた。
大きな氷塊の
まつ四角なその肩からまづ、
虹になってゆらゆらかげる。

石榴(ざくろ)が割れた。爆竹(ばくちく)がはぜ飛んだ。
鬼どもは天の一角を飛ばされ、ふきよせられ、霧になつた。泡にな
　　つた。
浮雲になった。
ながされた鮮血で天をそめるため。

鬼の児の歌　　Oni no ko no uta

Ascension

This is the day war-protesters are executed.
Souls desert bodies felled by the gunshots
And ascend to heaven.
To tell of immoral injustice.

Ogres, also in sorrow, begin to melt
Starting from the icebergs
Of their square shoulders
To become rainbows, shimmering, shimmering, growing dim.

Pomegranates split. Firecrackers burst.
The ogres in a heavenly corner, blown up, blown together, turn into
    mist; into froth.
They've become floating clouds.
In order to dye the sky with the newly spilled blood.

1949. *Songs of the ogre's children*

蛾　Ⅱ

蛾はとぶ。月のふぶきのなか。──月はむらさき。月がかざり立てる樹氷。
月にとけこんだ夜のしづかさ。蛾のやはらかい翼どもの、ふれあふ騒擾の無言のにぎやかさ。

鏡にふりつもるお白粉のやうに、蛾がふるひおとす鱗、紛々たる死よ。
蠟よりもすきとほつて千年もかはることのない若さの肌。

蛾はおもたい。さしわたしは一丈もある。無数に蛾のあつまつてゐるきよらかさは、
どんな穢(けがれ)ないこゝろで記された頁よりもあかるい。
ヌーヱル・エロイーズよりも。對話篇よりも、

煌々としたその明るさを僕はゆく。湖のながい汀にそうて、
はてしもしらずつゞく蛾のしかばねの柔らかさをふんで。
かへつてくることのない際涯をめざして。

蛾　*Ga*

Moths II

Moths fly. In the snowstorm of the moon. —The moon is purple. The moon adorns trees with silvery frost.
The quiet of the night melts into the moon. The silent excitement of moths' gentle wings busily touching one another.

Moths shake off scaly dust like face powder piling on a mirror—dust of death.
Youthful skin more translucent than wax, unaffected by a thousand years.

Moths are heavy. Their wingspan is as wide as a man's height. The limpidity of a gathering of innumerable moths
Is more illuminating than any pages written by the most innocent hearts
Than Nouvelle Heloise, than Plato's Dialogues.

I walk in the sparkling illumination, along the long shore of the lake
Treading on the softness of dead moths stretched out without end
Toward the remotest land that promises me no return.

1948. *Moths*

蛾 III

月に揉まれた湖。月にたましひをぬかれて、うつけになったから松
　の林。
月のぬけ毛のほそ雲。月の涙のころがりしづむ砂のやさしさ。
もはや、僕も、一ひらの月の影でしかないのだ。

僕が待ってゐる君、君はどこにゐる。月にさらはれたのか。月に消
　されたのか。
どこにも君はゐない。だがどこかおもひがけぬところで君は照り輝
　やかう。
月がてらす川底の美玉のやうに。

君によって天にかよふみちがひらけたのに！　純愛の寂寥さよ。
月にのぼりゆく泡沫とたはむれる、地上の愛慾に染まない死の天
　使、君によって。
月のレントゲンは、人間のいやらしい骸骨をゑがき出すかはりに、
砥ぎすました夜穹に、うつくしい汗の蒸溜の眞珠色の霧の一ひら
　を、
レースのやうにかるがると飛ばせる。

蛾　*Ga*

Moths III

The lake mauled by the moon. A grove of lifeless larches, their souls
    stolen by the moon.
The moon's fallen hair, thin strips of cloud. The moon's tears roll and
    seep into the sand's softness.
I, too, am after all a mere sliver of the moon's shadow.

Where are you? You, for whom I am waiting. Did the moon kidnap
    you? Did the moon erase you?
You are nowhere to be seen. But in the least imagined place you will
    glow and shine.
Like a jewel on the river bottom hit by the moonlight.

Because of you a passage has opened to heaven! Yet how forsaken it
    is, this innocent love!
Because of you, angel of death, free of earthly desires, toying with
    froth rising to the moon.
X-rays of the moon, instead of showing sickening human skeletons,
Let fly a single leaf of pearly mist
Distilled from beautiful sweat
Like weightless lace across the honed arch of night.

1948. *Moths*

球

ゆがみのない球の
ゆがんだ影。

燭の火心のやうに
銀とあこや貝の
ゆれてあそぶ中心。

しばしもとどまらぬ
無窮の廻轉の
やすらかさ。

弾力のあるあったかい頬の
ひやつこい表面。

しなやかになでる繻子の
月の光は辷る。

快い球よ。
たのしい球よ。

その球とともに
ころがる星空。

その球の奥に住む
白ゆりの花。

僕は疲れてゐる。
人間のことをかたるのは
ものうい。

Globe

The warped shadow
of a perfect sphere.

At its core silver and nacre
sway and play
like the wick of a candle.

Peacefulness
of a ceaseless
eternal orbit.

Cool surface
of warm resilient cheeks.

The moonlight glides—
a lithe satiny caress.

Pleasant sphere!
Joyful sphere!

The starry sky spins
with the sphere.

A white lily lives
in the depth of the sphere.

I am drained
I am weary of
talking of men.

ほかののぞみもなくて
こどものやうに、
球をみあげ
球をもてあそぶ。

永遠に若いもの
疲れをしらないものを
疲れたものが
ながめるたのしさ。

快い球よ。
たのしい球よ。

僕の夢のなかで
ころがる球の
とりわけ自由自在なこと。

あゝ、上天にはもはや
神も、天使もゐまさず、
球と球があそぶだけ。

大小の球は
もつれ、かさなり
ひゞきを立てて
喨々とうたふ。

昇天とは、球と球との
終始ない凸と凹とのつながりを
蟻のやうにはてしもしらず
よぢのぼってゆくことだ。

蛾　*Ga*

Having nothing else to hope for
I look up at the globe
like a child
I toy with the globe.

Joy for the fatigued
to gaze
at the eternally young
who know no fatigue.

Pleasant Sphere!
Joyful Sphere!

How carefree above all
is the spinning sphere
in my dreams.

Ah, God and angels
no longer reside in heaven
only spheres play with spheres.

Small and large spheres
entangle, pile up
clang with one another, and
sonorously sing.

Ascension is to climb
like an ant not knowing the end
up the seamless link of concave and convex
of sphere to sphere.

1948. *Moths*

雨

むすぼれた雨が
しづかに林に湧き
苔みどりの湖に
白い繭(まゆ)をかける。

吸入器の噴霧のやうに
いがらつぽい
毒つぽい雨。

ぱらぱらこぼれてくる
葉のしづく。
葉うらにびっしり
貼りついてゐる蛾の卵。

青虫を餌食にして、
草や木は青々とひろがる。
裳(も)のやうに。
袖のやうに。

ぬれた草を倒して
ふみぬいたパンツのやうに
蛇が匍(は)ふ。
パンツをぬぐ腰のやうに。

あまり長雨がつゞくので
僕のこころは水びたしだ。
そらにも大きな
壁じみができた。

Rain

Dismal rain
quietly wells up in the woods
casting a white cocoon
over the moss-green lake.

Rain
nasty and noxious
like vapor from an inhaler.

Drops flutter down
from leaves.
their undersides are densely covered
with moth eggs.

Preying on caterpillars
grass and trees thrive in lush green.
like a skirt.
like a sleeve.

A snake crawls
pushing over wet grass
like a pair of pants someone stepped out of.
like his hips getting out of the pants.

It has been raining for so long
that my heart is soaked.
the sky also has
large water-stains.

浮袋よ。どこかへ浮びあがらせろ。
毎日、頭をおさへつける
こんないやな周囲から、
あっちもこっちも浮腫(ふしゅ)だらけだぜ。

生きてるといふことは何ですか。先生。
君、それは何かでふくれてることだよ。
では、わるいことなんですか。
ふん。まあ、うつたうしいことさね。

ぬれた障子。
しとつた畳に坐つて僕の魂は
生きてゐればこその偏執と食慾と、
青かび、黒かびに蔽(おほ)はれてゐる。

こんな日にはまつたく
男だつて懐胎(くわいたい)しますよ。
きこえないか。この胎動が
罪の児がうごいてゐるのが。

〈昭和二〇・七〉

蛾　*Ga*

Floating tube, float me up to somewhere!
away from this hateful place
which oppresses my mind
edema is spreading all around.

Professor, what does it mean to live?
It means being bloated with something.
Is it, then, something bad?
Um, well, it's depressing, you see.

A wet sliding paper door.
my soul sits on damp tatami mats
covered by paranoia and hunger as proofs of being alive
covered by blue and black mold.

On a day like this
even a guy can conceive
Can't you hear? This quickening—
a fetus of sin is moving.

(July 1945)

1948. *Moths*

富士

重箱のやうに
狭つくるしいこの日本。

すみからすみまでみみつちく
俺達は数えあげられてゐるのだ。

そして、失禮千萬にも
俺達を召集しやがるんだ。

戸籍簿よ。早く焼けてしまへ。
誰も。俺の息子をおぼえてるな。

息子よ。
この手のひらにもみこまれてゐろ。
帽子のうらへ一時、消えてゐろ。

父と母とは、裾野の宿で
一晩ぢゆう、そのことを話した。

裾野の枯林をぬらして
小枝をピシピシ折るやうな音を立てて
夜どほし、雨がふってゐた。

息子よ。づぶぬれになったお前が
重たい銃を曳きずりながら、喘ぎながら
自失したやうにあるいてゐる。それはどこだ?

Mount Fuji

Like a stacked-up lunch box
our Japan is cramped and confined.

From one corner to the other
we are stingily tallied up.

And they are so inexcusably rude,
they draft us into the military.

Census Books, go up in flames!
Forget my son, and everyone else.

Son,
roll yourself up into my palm
get lost in my cap for a while.

All night long in a lodge in Mount Fuji's foothills
your mother and father talked about this.

It rained through the night
soaking the bare trees in the foothills
making noises like twigs snapping.

My son, you are drenched
dragging a heavy gun, panting
as if you've lost yourself. Where are you?

どこだかわからない。が、そのお前を
父と母とがあてどなくさがしに出る
そんな夢ばかりのいやな一夜が
長い、不安な夜がやつと明ける。

雨はやんでゐる。
息子のゐないうつろな空に
なんだ。糞面白くもない
あらひざらした浴衣のやうな
富士。

蛾　*Ga*

We didn't know where, but
your mother and father set out aimlessly looking for you
such nightmares fill the loathsome night
the long anxious night is finally giving way.

The rain has stopped.
in the vacant sky where my son is not
Mount Fuji is
like a frayed and faded robe
to hell with it.

1948. Moths

雪

　鼠いろの雪が
もぞもぞとそこらを這ふ。

空間を攀ぢのぼって
雪は
空をうづめ、

掠めては消える雪の屑、
こまかい、かるい粉雪が、
ふかさの底に
おちこんだしづかさで、
東、西、南、北を閉す。

もつとふれ。雪よ。
もつと、もつと、もつと。
雪の重みでおしつぶされる小屋のなかに、
父と、子の母と、子の三人が、
ほだ火をかこんでうづくまる。
隣家とは五丁も隔たつてゐる。
このへだたりがなにより安堵。
雪よ。もつとふれ。もつと積れ。

雪よ。虱のやうに
世界にはびこれ。
すべての連絡を杜絶せよ。
そして、音信不通にしろ。

Snow

    Rat-colored antsy snow
creeps about all around.

Climbing up into the air
snow
fills the sky,

Snow-dust slinks by and disappears
powdery snow fine and light
falls to the bottom of the depths. The quiet
closes off East, West, South, and North.

Snow, come down more
more, more, more.
In a shack pressed under the weight of snow
son, father, and mother—three
huddle together by a wood fire.
The nearest neighbor is as much as 500 meters away.
This distance provides peace of mind above all.
Snow, come down more, pile up more.

Snow, proliferate like lice
all over the world.
Cut off all communication
and render the world silent.

電話も、手紙もここへはやつてくるな。
戦争の報道や、
暴力からこの父をまもれ。
見識のない弱蟲な、幇間文士の誘ひから
母の耳をふさいでやれ。

それから、もつとかんじんなことは
きいても嘔気のくる赤紙が
子の手元へは届かないやうに、
雪よ。八尺も、十尺もふれ。

蛾　*Ga*

Don't come here, telephones or letters.
Keep father safe from violence
and the news of war.
Close mother's ears
keep her from the lures of stupid, cowardly, groveling writers.

What's more, most important of all,
keep the nauseating red slip of a draft notice
from reaching our child,
You, snow! Pile up eight feet, ten feet high.

1948. *Moths*

霧

　どこから流れてきて、
どこへおしよせるのだ。
霧よ。
湖水をのみ
から松林を喰ひちぎり
みんな、腹の袋につめこむ霧。

僕があるいてゐると
落葉の小路が、たちまち
先も、あともみえなくなって
僕は、立止る。

僕の生きてきたうしろも、前も
濃霧よ。
葬ってくれたんだね。

傍らを人がすれちがっても、
僕といふことがわからない。
足音がひびいて、近づいてきて
ぼんやりとした人の影が
あらはれたかとおもふと、すっと消える。

僕がやってきたことの汚鮎(しみ)。
破廉恥なわが顔つきを
僕はもう、二度とみたくない。
つながる過去の人人とも
あひたくない。聲もききたくない。

FOG

Where do you flow in from
And where do you push on to?
Fog!
You swallow the lake
Tear away the grove of larches
Bag them all in your belly.

As I walk
The leaf-strewn path ahead of or behind me
Instantly becomes invisible
I pause.

Deep Fog, for me
You've buried
What is ahead and behind in the passage of my life, haven't you?

Even people passing right by me
Won't know it's me.
Footsteps sound, come closer
A vague human figure
Appears and disappears just as fast.

The stains of what I have done.
I don't want to ever see
My shameless face again.
I don't want to meet nor hear the voices of
Those who connect me to the past.

ああ、できるなら、霧よ。消してくれ。
この霧の奥から、僕の人生が、
ふたたびぬけぬけと浮び上って来ないやうに
僕も、周囲も、この世紀のいやな出来事も、
林檎のくされを
ナイフでえぐってすてるやうに
やさしくて、きびしい霧よ。
切り取ってくれ。消してくれ。

蛾　*Ga*

Ah, if you could, dear Fog, obliterate
Me, my surroundings, and the hateful events of this century
So that my life won't brazenly rise up again
From the depths of this fog.
Just as one gouges out with a knife
The rotten part of an apple.
Gentle yet unflinching Fog!
Gouge them out. Obliterate them.

1948. *Moths*

―自敍傳について

いつからか幕があいて
僕が生きはじめてゐた。
僕の頭上には空があり
青瓜よりも青かった。

ここを日本だとしらぬ前から
やぶれ障子が立つてゐて
日本人の父と母とが
しょんぼり畳に坐ってゐた。

茗荷の子や、蕗のたうがにほふ。
匂ひはくまなくくぐり入り
いちばん遠い、いちばん仄かな
記憶を僕らにつれもどす。

おもへは、生きつづけたものだ。
もはやだいたいわかりきった
おなじやうな明日ばかりで
大それた過ちも起りさうもない。

いつのまにか、僕にも妻子がゐて
友人、知人、若干にかこまれ
どこの港をすぎたのかも
気にとめぬうちに、月日がすぎた。

そのうち、はこばれてきたところが
こんな寂しい日本国だった。
はりまぜの汚れ屏風に圍はれて
僕は一人、焼跡で眼をさました。

人間の悲劇　*Ningen no higeki*

—On Autobiography

I don't know when it was but the curtain rose and
I was beginning to live.
There was the sky above me
bluer than an unripe gourd.

Before I learned I was in Japan
tattered *shōji* stood
Mother and Father, Japanese,
sat on tatami mats, crestfallen.

I smell flower buds of ginger and butterburs.
The smell sneaks in to permeate the air
bringing back the most distant and the faintest
of memories.

To think how I've survived—
All I'll have will be only tomorrows as before
mostly as expected
I don't expect bad mistakes either.

By and by I also had a family
surrounded by a few friends and acquaintances
time went by
while paying no attention to what ports we sailed past.

In the end, I was brought here
to this desolate country of Japan.
Surrounded by dingy patched-up folding screens
I awoke, alone, in the fire-ravaged land.

1952. *Tragedy of man*

"On Autobiography" is the opening verse of No. 2 in *Ningen no higeki* (Tragedy of man), a book-length work in ten parts that mixes verse and prose.—Trans.

心

こころは、いつも半開きのまゝになってゐた。出口とおもって、踏み
　　こんでから
吹きこむ土砂のうづだかい、荒廢のさまを見廻して、踵(くびす)をか
　　へすものもあり、

また、氣づかずにゆきすぎるものも多かったが、僕は
いまは、この座よりやすらかなところはどこにもなく、たとへば、男
　　根のかたちを軒先にかかげ

古壁にみだらな落書のある、ここが立ちぐされの妓樓のあととわか
　　つても、
變哲もない。つめたい壁の片隅に、僕が膝を立て、

芥蜘蛛のやうにわが身をうづくまれば、いつのまにやら、足音も立
　　てずおづおづと
手まはりをもつた浮浪者どもが同類をもとめ、一人、また、一人と、
　　僕のまはりに寄ってきて坐る。

非情　*Hijō*

HEART

My heart has always been left half open. Some people step in,
    thinking it's an exit,
look around over barren piles of sand blowing in, and turn on their
    heels,

Many just pass by without noticing it, but as for me,
I now have no restful place other than this, and if, for example,
    I realize

this is the remains of a dilapidated brothel with a carved phallus
    hanging under the eave,
with lewd graffiti on its decrepit walls, no matter. In a chilly corner
    of the walls, my knees drawn up,

I curl up like an orb-weaver; then before I realize it,
vagrants, timidly, soundlessly, come carrying their bare necessities,
    seeking kindred, one by one, and sit around me.

1955. Heartless

葦（あし）

　水から空へ
いつぽんの葦が立つ。
葦は、ふるへる。
まっすぐな茎から

葉の末端までが
こまかにふるへる。
突つ立つたまゝ投箭（なげや）が
ふるへてゐるやうに。

まみづと
しほみづのなかで
ゆられる葦は
ねたり起きたりしながら

ふなべりをこすり
舟のあふりで
うちひろがる波紋が、
なかば、水につかって

ねむってゐる
千本、万本の葦を
つぎつぎに
ざわめかせる。

あゝ、ことしほど
秋の水が
こゝろと目にしみた
ことはなかった。

Reeds

From water to the sky
a single reed stands.
The reed trembles.
From its straight stalk

to the tip of its leaves
it is subtly shaking
like a dart quivers
straight up.

Reeds swaying
in clear water
and salt water
lie down and rise

rub the sides of a boat
which stirs and spreads
ripples
forcing

thousands and tens of thousands of reeds
half in water, asleep
to rustle
one after another.

Ah, I've never had
water in autumn
affect my heart and eyes
as it does this year.

水底にひたされた
葦の根をおしわけて
水のにほひの
いざなふままに、

舟と僕は、すゝむ。
ちぎれちぎれに
とぶ雲のしたを、
ひろがる水のうへを。

けふまで僕を揃(つかま)へてゐた
五十何年のながさから
とき放された僕を
小舟は、はこび

小舟はたゞよひ
僕をあそばせる。
舟ぞこにねそべつて
僕は、おもふ。

僕からながれ去った
五十何年は
葦洲(あしす)のむかうに
渺茫(べうぼう)とつづいて

けぢめもつかない。
それにしても
なにがあつた。
どんなことが。

Pushing apart the roots of reeds
soaked at the bottom of water
as the smell of water
lures

the boat and I move forward
under the clouds
broken in flight
over the expanse of water.

The small boat carries
me released
from fifty-some long years
that have confined me until today and

the boat is adrift
letting me idle along.
Lying at the bottom of the boat
I ponder.

Fifty-some years
that have drained out of me
extend far into the vast
flat of reeds and

no end in sight.
Even so
what happened?
what sort of things?

水のながれにも似た
時のながれにおされ、
ゆく水の、おもひもかけぬ
底のはやさにさらはれ、

愛憎の
もつれのまゝに
うきつ、しづみつ、
なにをみるひまも僕にはなかった。

しかし、おどろく程のことはない。
女たちの
やさしさ以外は
みんなつまらないことばかりだ。

葦の葉から
葦の葉へ
ぬけてゆく風のやうに、みんな
こけおどかしにすぎないのだ。

コップに挿(さ)した
花茎のやうに
ほそうでをまげて
ふふと、笑ひかける女、

僕からついと身を避けて、
ふりむきもせず、流れていつた
ゆきずりの女。
女たちは、みんな花だった。

Pressed by the passage of time
like flowing water
swept up by the surprising momentum
of moving water at its deepest.

I had no time to see anything
I bobbed up and down
as love and hate
entangled.

But no big deal.
Other than women's
tenderness
all is tedious.

Like a breeze moving through
from leaves of reeds
to leaves of reeds
everything is a mere charade.

A woman giggled at me
bending her slender arm
like a flower stem
put into a glass.

A woman in passing
swiftly skirted me and
did not look back, drifting on.
The women were all flowers.

水は、
それをはこんだ。
どこへ。
それはしらない。

五十何年が
ながれ去ったあとの
からからになつた僕の
なんといふかるさ。

なんといふあかるさ。
水のうへをゆく心に、さあ
きいてみるがい〻。
つゆほどの反逆がのこつてゐるかと。

非情　*Hijō*

Water
carried them
to where?
I don't know where.

How weightless I feel
now that I have dried up
as fifty-some years
have flown away.

How luminous!
Just ask
my heart riding on water
if it has even a bit of rebellion left.

1955. Heartless

MIYOSHI TATSUJI
三好達治

Miyoshi Tatsuji
(1900–1964)

LIFE AND CAREER

Miyoshi Tatsuji's childhood was marked by traumatic dislocations in his living arrangements, which produced episodes of debilitating existential fear in this uncommonly bright and sensitive boy. Later in life, when he had found comfort in poetry and literature, a desperate feeling of being lost and a yearning for love characterized many of his poems. His finest poems were masterly expressions of the intimate connection between external reality and the inner workings of the human mind. His ability to elevate elements from everyday life into matters of transcendent import gives his work a power not often found in lyrical poetry.

Miyoshi was born in Osaka as the oldest of ten children in a family that ran a small printing business. To reduce the number of mouths to feed, when he was six his parents put him up for adoption by a family in Kyoto, but the law prohibited adoption of a first-born boy. Instead he was sent to live with his grandparents. He enrolled in a local elementary school near their home, but at age eight he was "tormented by fears of death and being alone through the night," resulting in a breakdown, "which made him unable to attend school for a long time."[1] Three years later he rejoined his birth parents and attended their local elementary school, only to have the fears of death and loneliness recur when he was thirteen. It was at this time that he started

---

1. Miyoshi, *Zenshishū*, 748.

frequenting the public library with a classmate and reading popular contemporary novels.

Miyoshi started writing haiku at fourteen while attending Osaka's municipal middle school. When he was fifteen he had to leave middle school because of his parents' financial problems. Honoring his father's wishes, he took and passed a difficult entrance examination for the military academy in Osaka in order to get a free education. At nineteen he was dispatched as an officer candidate to Army Engineering Battalion 19, which was stationed in northern Korea. While serving there he studied and excelled in French and *kendō* (traditional swordsmanship). He then went on to Army Officers' School to be trained as a full officer. While in the officers' school he secretly read the Bible and Marx's *Das Kapital*, which he later wrote that he did not understand at all. He also continued his studies in French, and read *tanka* and contemporary lyric poetry. By this time he had composed over a thousand haiku, written down in his notebook. But after only one year he dropped out of the officers' school because, as he later recalled, "I was by nature not suited for a military career, and also I lacked the military spirit."[2]

Miyoshi worked briefly to help his father's business, but it was not doing well so he went to stay with his aunt, who supported Miyoshi financially so he could attend the Third National School of Higher Education in Kyoto in 1922 and pursue his interests. He majored in literature and forged friendships with some fellow students who would later become leading thinkers and writers. The young Miyoshi was especially drawn to the lyrical poetry of Hagiwara Sakutarō and Murō Saisei. At this point he was writing very little poetry of his own, although he demonstrated sharp critical insight in discussions with his friends. He also started reading Nietzsche, Schopenhauer, Turgenev, and others. He particularly admired Turgenev, "much more so than Tolstoy, Chekov, and Dostoyevsky,"[3] as he later wrote.

---

2. Ibid., 751.
3. Ibid., 752.

Upon graduation from the National School of Higher Education in 1925 he was admitted to Tokyo Imperial University, where he majored in French literature. Lectures on Mallarmé and Baudelaire made a strong impression on him, and he wrote "On Paul Verlaine's *Sagasse*" as his graduation thesis. While at the university he devotedly read almost all the works of the Japanese lyrical poets of the time, memorizing several hundred of their poems. He joined the coterie magazine *Aozora* (Blue sky) with fellow alumni from the Third National School of Higher Education. The poems he published in *Aozora* received high praise from the editor of another coterie magazine, *Shii no ki* (Beech tree), which he was also invited to join. His poetry was published frequently in these magazines, and he formed close friendships with young aspiring poets at the university. A year before graduation he visited Hagiwara Sakutarō, who became his "one and only"[4] mentor in poetry. Hagiwara took Miyoshi to meet Murō Saisei, a gesture that in effect bridged two generations of lyrical poets.

After graduating from Tokyo Imperial University in 1928 Miyoshi set out to be a writer. That year he was a founding member of *Shi to shiron* (Poetry and poetics), which published his poetry as well as his translations of and essays on French poets. While he wrote a great deal of poetry and many essays, he earned his living as a prolific translator of French verse and prose, including the works of Baudelaire, Paul Valéry, Verlaine, Rimbaud, and Francis Jammes, as well as Jean-Henri Fabre's *Entomological Souvenirs*.

Miyoshi's first book of poetry, *Sokuryōsen* (Surveyor ship), published in 1930, earned him recognition as a representative lyrical poet. He also produced three collections of four-line poems, *Nansō shū* (Poems from the south window) (1932), *Kanka shū* (Poems in the quiet) (1934), and *Sanka shū* (Mountain fruits) (1935), as well as a collection of *tanka* in 1934. That was the year the poetry magazine *Shiki* was reestablished as a monthly with Miyoshi, Hori Tatsuo, and Maruyama Kaoru as coeditors. *Shiki* gradually expanded its roster

---

4. Miyoshi Tatsuji, *Miyoshi Tatsuji, Nihon shijin zenshū 21* (Miyoshi Tatsuji: Complete collection of Japanese poets vol. 21) (Tokyo: Shinchōsha, 1967), 288.

of members and contributors. Its fifteenth issue in 1936 pronounced its purpose as "to uphold the superior tradition of Japanese poetry and to develop new poetry for the future,"[5] echoing the nationalistic attitude of the time. *Shiki* thrived, providing a forum for creative energy during the most turbulent years in modern Japanese history, and was an overwhelmingly powerful presence in modern Japanese poetry until it ended in 1944. As an editor and contributor to *Shiki*, Miyoshi was central to the pursuit of lyrical poetry, which provided common ground for poets struggling to survive under the ultra-nationalistic demands of the military regime. At the same time Miyoshi published three books of poems in praise of victories at war, or of military readiness and resolve to win the war, between 1942 and 1944. These were mostly written in forceful and archaic diction and rhythms, though some of them evoked bygone days of peace and elegance. Miyoshi was not only highly respected by fellow poets as an editor and writer, but also very popular among general readers.

After the war Miyoshi wrote a series of essays about his beloved Japan in which he questioned the Emperor's moral responsibility for the conduct of the war, and even suggested his abdication. This triggered vocal criticism, notably from Ayukawa Nobuo, who led the postwar poetry movement *Arechi*. Ayukawa accused him of hypocrisy, pointing to Miyoshi's wartime poems in praise of nationalism and military victories. Younger postwar poets joined in to reject not only Miyoshi's wartime poetry, but all of his poetry, as well as all of the other poets associated with *Shiki*, as "the *Shiki* group," in effect dismissing lyricism in modern poetry. From a twenty-first century vantage point, the question remains whether it was reasonable for these younger poets to castigate Miyoshi as a mortal enemy of their new poetics, even while it must be admitted that this youthful uprising to reject the past in order to create a poetics for the new age delivered significant results. This is especially true given the fact that many of Miyoshi's wartime poems can be read as symbolic presentations of

---

5. Miyoshi, *Zenshishū*, 769.

the pain of having to endure the world as it was. For example, "Crow" depicts an unreasonable submission to an unseen yet almighty power. "Family" presents the quiet sorrow of a writer, the breadwinner of the family, who sends off his first-grader son with newly bought school supplies to the entrance ceremony of a People's School, in which "People" signifies "subjects of the Emperor." The more famous and popular a poet was, the stronger was the pressure on him or her to produce work promoting the nationalist cause. Was it really possible for a prominent poet of the time to deny such demands? That is a question the aspiring young poets did not have to face. Instead they were mobilized to the battleground and forced to take part in Imperialist aggression as unhappy participants. Both old and young were equally victimized by the totalitarian regime.

It took some time before the impassioned rejection of the younger generation was replaced by a reasoned reevaluation of Miyoshi's work and of lyricism in general. Even during this stressful period, however, Miyoshi continued to be widely regarded as a great poet in Japan, with an enthusiastic readership. Two of his books of poetry, *Kokyō no hana* (Flowers of my hometown) and *Suna no toride* (Fortress of sand), were published as early as 1946. *Rakuda no kobu ni matagatte* (Straddling the camel's hump), his last published book of poetry, appeared in 1952.

Miyoshi received the Geijutsuin shō (Art Academy Award) in 1953 in recognition of his entire body of work and his contribution to the development of modern poetry. *Teihon Miyoshi Tatsuji shishū* (Authorized complete poems of Miyoshi Tatsuji), from which Miyoshi excluded most of his openly prowar poetry, was published in 1962, receiving that year's Yomiuri Literary Award. He died of a heart attack in April of 1964. Chikuma shobō started publishing the twelve-volume *Miyoshi Tatsuji zenshū* (Collected works of Miyoshi Tatsuji) shortly after his death, completing the collection in 1966.

POETRY

Miyoshi's first book of poetry, *Sokuryōsen* (Surveyor ship), consists mostly of poems written in the modern vernacular. The exceptions were pieces that use classic verbiage designed to evoke a long-ago past. The language is clean, crisp, and lucid, presenting actions and movements in a logical sequence, yet evoking a deeper layer that suggests a hidden drama. Each poem is composed in a particular rhythm—fluid and dreamy in one, crisp and tense in another—that creates an ambiance, emotional state, and insight specific to the world of that poem. In "The Youth," for example, each line is carefully measured to conjure an image of a youth going home, not hurrying, in the deepening dusk. He comes out of a monastery, tossing a ball as he walks along the tree-lined pathway, heading for home under a sky that flows like a dream. The voice of the poem is omniscient, leaving readers alone with the youth. Is this alluring youth real, or is he a phantom in a dream? Is he really on his way home, or is he an image of one's own youth to which one wishes to return? The possibilities are intriguing, each implying a haunting drama.

Compare this to "Crow," which is also written in the vocabulary and the rhythm of normal speech, but to completely different effect. In a sequence of precise and orderly descriptions, the man's fear and discomfort quickly build as the reader empathizes with the mounting psychological conflict and tension of a man being forced to follow bizarre orders from the sky that will turn him into a crow, flying endlessly and obediently. No matter how we read this poem, whether as a tale of inner personal conflict or as a premonition of oppressive times to come, Miyoshi constructs a powerful symbolic reality that is not bound to any specific time or place.

In 1940 Miyoshi wrote an essay in which he touches on the shift in his poetic style: "[F]or a long time I wrote poetry as if sketching a still-life—efficiently, in one breath, on a charcoal paper with carbon ... But now I pursue music in poetry, or what one might call the music of words, the tactile texture of words, backed by old-fashioned but solid stereophonic effects filled with sensations, or with overflowing consciousness."⁶ Miyoshi's statement of this shift in his poetic style from clean and straightforward wording to a pursuit of musicality in poetry in this particular timeframe was significant. It was when Japan was in pursuit of hegemony over Southeast Asia, and on the brink of the attack on Pearl Harbor that opened the Pacific war. In other words, it was a time when the military regime's censorship of literature was unreasonably intense and poets found themselves having to avoid straight talk lest they attract unwanted attention.

In an environment where imperial power rested on the ancient creation myth of the land, it was understandable that the grace and elegance of ancient times were a safe haven for many. In his pursuit of musicality Miyoshi evoked the imagined elegance and peace of the past in a modified traditional cadence. This effect is seen in poems such as "May the *Koto*'s Resonance Soar," which carries the reader into a quaint world of its own, away from times when "warriors are fighting many battles." Its evocation of a dreamy world through traditional music lifts the reader out of reality. "Call My Name" is also written in archaic diction, in a flowing yet irregular rhythm, which effectively creates urgency out of despair. The poem grips the reader with an intense yearning for a comforting voice from childhood that is now forever lost. Was this loss caused by war, or by some other unfortunate fate? No matter. Fate has left the speaker all alone by the tea bush in the cold wind and snow.

During this same period Miyoshi also published poems praising the war effort, celebrating news of victorious battles, or lamenting the loss of a leading general. In many of these he conveyed a staccato military marching beat through the use of Chinese ideograms, which, when used in the Japanese language, are short in sound, and square in their visual impression.

His postwar poems changed style once again. He wrote free verse in contemporary language, with clear and crisp diction, carefully or-

---

6. Ibid., 777. Taken from Miyoshi's essay "A Journey of a Soul" (1940) and quoted in the detailed chronology of Miyoshi's career.

dered to generate the desired effect. His eyes were again focused on reality, presented in a straightforward manner. "Stirring in Me Seems" shows an aged man in a war-torn cityscape, vaguely recalling and feeling the returning spring, pondering and heavy-hearted, yet somehow anticipating a renewal. His dejected and muddled mindscape is conveyed through careful use of the colloquial language. The reader hears the man mumble, and with no warning, the voice of the poem shifts to omniscient accounts of the source of the mumblings and the man's history and surroundings. At times these internal and external viewpoints converge, blurring the border between the old man's mindscape, his feelings, and the world around him, which strikes the reader with an awareness of the degree of devastation and despair the war caused him. Miyoshi's poetry invites readers to experience its reality and its psyche, and then to peer into their own minds, into the depths of humanity, to see truth. Tanikawa Shuntarō, a leading poet of the generation after Miyoshi, had this to say about his mentor:

> [A]t the heart of Miyoshi's poetry is something fleeting yet eternal, something totally of no [practical] use yet directly touching the mysteries of our life, or a miniscule light equally inherent in brightness and darkness. This something is felt, and is tempting us to seize it, at the depths (or pinnacles) of life that are the hardest areas to explore. Even Time, a form of consciousness we can never escape, is on the brink of collapse. This is true even when his work presents seemingly pleasant mundane matters of daily life. However small a life or an object it describes, his poetry presents it as part of the mutually referencing structural elements of an organic entity called the world. This allows a penetrating view of an infinite expanse as large as the universe itself. That is the greatness of Miyoshi's poetry.[7]

In his poem "Self Portrait" Miyoshi says, "Sky's winged vagrants / Meet here // I am rent-free lodging / Angels come. Owls arrive // I give you courtesy passes / Sleep here ... ." While he nurtured and sustained

---

7. Tanikawa Shuntarō, ed., *Miyoshi Tatsuji shishū, Sekai no shi* 26 (Selected poems of Miyoshi Tatsuji: poetry of the world vol. 26) (Tokyo: Yayoishobō, 1965), 165.

a huge current of lyrical poetry in Japan through difficult times, Miyoshi is not a simple lyrical poet. His creative genius constructs a world of its own that invites a reader to share an experience and to discover a critical moment of truth in life, however fleeting it might be.

少年

夕ぐれ
とある精舎(しやうじゃ)の門から
美しい少年が歸つてくる

暮れやすい一日(いちにち)に
てまりをなげ
空高くてまりをなげ
なほも遊びながら歸つてくる

閑静な街の
人も樹も色をしづめて
空は夢のやうに流れてゐる

測量船　*Sokuryōsen*

The Youth

The day is ending
Out of a monastery gate
An alluring youth is coming home

He tosses a ball
Up into the day closing fast
Tossing it high into the sky
Still playing as he comes home

In a quiet street
People and trees appear in subdued colors
The sky flows like dreams

1930. *Surveyor ship*

湖水

この湖水で人が死んだのだ
それであんなにたくさん舟が出てゐるのだ

葦(あし)と藻草(もぐさ)の　どこに死骸はかくれてしまったのか

それを見出した合圖(あひづ)の笛はまだ鳴らない

風が吹いて　水を切る艪(ろ)の音櫂(かい)の音
風が吹いて　草の根や蟹の匂ひがする

ああ誰かがそれを知ってゐるのか
この湖水で夜明けに人が死んだのだと

誰かがほんとに知ってゐるのか
もうこんなに夜が來てしまったのに

測量船　*Sokuryōsen*

The Lake

A person died in this lake
That is why so many boats are out there

Where in the reeds and water weeds is the body hiding?
A whistle signaling its discovery is yet to be heard

The wind blows; I hear the sound of oars and paddles cutting the water
The wind blows; I smell crabs and roots of grass

Ah, does someone know that
A person died in this lake at dawn?

Does someone really know that?
Night has come over us

1930. *Surveyor ship*

村

鹿は角に麻縄をしばられて、暗い物置小屋にいれられてゐた。何も見えないところで、その青い眼はすみ、きちんと風雅に坐ってゐた。芋が一つころがつてゐた。

そとでは櫻の花が散り、山の方から、ひとすぢそれを自轉車がしいていつた。背中を見せて、少女は藪を眺めてゐた。羽織の肩に、黒いリボンをとめて。

測量船　*Sokuryōsen*

A Village

The deer was held in a dark shed, tied by the horns with a hempen rope. He sat neatly, gracefully, where he couldn't see anything, his blue eyes clear. A single taro was lying there.

Outside, cherry trees were cascading petals, covering the ground. A bicycle came down from the hills, leaving a single track through them. A girl was gazing at the thicket, her back to me, a black ribbon fastened on the shoulder of her kimono coat.

1930. *Surveyor ship*

鴉

　風の早い曇り空に太陽のありかも解らない日の、人けない一すぢの道の上に私は涯しない野原をさまようてゐた。風は四方の地平から私を呼び、私の袖を捉へ裾をめぐり、そしてまたその荒まじい叫び聲をどこかへ消してしまふ。その時私はふと枯草の上に捨てられてある一枚の黒い上衣を見つけた。私はまたどこからともなく私に呼びかける聲を聞いた。

　　　——とまれ！

　私は立ちどまって周圍に聲のありかを探した。私は恐怖を感じた。

　　　——お前の着物を脱げ！

　恐怖の中に私は羞恥と微かな憤りを感じながら、餘儀なくその命令の言葉に從った。するとその聲はなほ冷やかに、

　　　——裸になれ！　その上衣を拾って着よ！

　と、もはや抵抗しがたい威嚴を帶びて、草の間から私に命じた。私は惨めな姿に上衣を羽織って風の中に曝されてゐた。私の心は敗北に用意をした。

　　　——飛べ！

　しかし何といふ奇異な、思ひがけない言葉であらう。私は自分の手足を顧みた。手は長い翼になって兩腋に疊まれ、鱗をならべた足は三本の指で石ころを踏んでゐた。私の心はまた服從の用意をした。

　　　——飛べ！

Crow

On a day when the sun was nowhere to be seen hiding behind the clouds in fierce wind, I was roaming in a boundless field along a deserted path. The wind called me from the four corners of the earth, catching my sleeves, skirting around my legs, and aimlessly dispersing its wild screams. Then I happened to catch sight of a black robe discarded on the withered grass. Once again I heard a voice calling to me from nowhere.

—Stop!

I stopped and looked to see where the voice was coming from. Fear gripped me.

—Take your clothes off!

In my fear, feeling shamed and a little angry, I could not help but follow the order. Then the voice came, even more chillingly,

—Get naked! Pick up the robe and wear it!

giving me orders from among the grasses, with a dignity I could not resist. I put the robe on my miserable self, and stood exposed to the wind. My mind was ready for a defeat.

—Fly!

What a strange, unexpected word! I looked at my arms and legs. My arms had grown into long wings and folded; scaled legs with three toes stood on the pebbles. My mind again readied itself for submission.

—Fly!

私は促されて土を蹴った。私の心は急に怒りに満ち溢れ、鋭い悲哀に貫かれて、ただひたすらにこの屈辱の地をあとに、あてもなく一直線に翔(かけ)つていつた。感情が感情に鞭うち、意志が意志に鞭うちながら——。私は永い時間を飛んでゐた。そしてもはや今、あの惨めな敗北からは遠く飛び去って、翼には疲労を感じ、私の敗北の祝福さるべき希望の空を夢みてゐた。それだのに、ああ！なほその時私の耳に近く聞えたのは、あの執拗な命令の聲ではなかつたか。

　　——啼け！

おお、今こそ私は啼くであらう。

　　——啼け！
　　——よろしい、私は啼く。

そして、啼きながら私は飛んでゐた。飛びながら私は啼いてゐた。

　　——ああ、ああ、ああ、ああ、
　　——ああ、ああ、ああ、ああ、

風が吹いてゐた。その風に秋が木葉をまくやうに私は言葉を撒いてゐた。冷めたいものがしきりに頬を流れてゐた。

測量船　*Sokuryōsen*

Urged on, I kicked up from the dirt. With my heart suddenly filled with anger, pierced by sharp sadness, I soared aimlessly into the air in a straight line, leaving behind this earth of humiliation. My feelings whipped my feelings; my will whipped my will ... I flew for a long time. I had flown far from that miserable humiliation, and felt fatigue in my wings, dreaming of a hopeful sky where my defeat should be celebrated. And yet, ah, what I heard was none other than the persistent voice of command.

—Caw!

Oh, now, I will caw.

—Caw!
—All right, I will caw.

And cawing, I flew. Flying I cawed.

—aah, aah, aah, aah
—aah, aah, aah, aah

The wind was blowing. I scattered my words into the wind just like Autumn scatters the leaves of trees. Something chilly kept flowing down my cheeks.

1930. *Surveyor ship*

信號

小舎の水車　藪かげに一株の椿
新らしい轍に蝶が下りる　それは向きをかへながら
静かな翼の抑揚に　私の歩みを押しとどめる
「踏切りよ　ここは……」　私は立ちどまる

南窓集　*Nansō shū*

Signal

A waterwheel by the mill. A lone camellia tree in the shade of a
    thicket
A butterfly flutters down to a newly made rut, moving in different
    directions
To the quiet rhythms of its wings—it arrests me
"Here we are, dear, the railroad crossing ..." I pause

1932. *Poems from the south window*

土

蟻が
蝶の羽をひいて行く
ああ
ヨットのやうだ

南窗集　*Nansō shū*

EARTH

An ant goes
dragging a butterfly wing
ah
like a yacht!

1932. *Poems from the south window*

仔羊

海の青さに耳をたて　圍ひの柵を跳び越える　仔羊
砂丘の上に馳けのぼり　己れの影にとび上る　仔羊よ
私の歌は　今朝生れたばかりの仔羊
潮の薫りに眼を瞬き　飛び去る雲の後を追ふ

山果集　*Sanka shū*

Lamb

Lamb,
you prick up your ears to the blue of the sea, leap over the surround-
 ing fence
trot up the sand dunes, and romp with your shadow
my song is this morning's newborn lamb
blinking its eyes at the scent of the tides, chasing after clouds that fly
 away

1935. *Mountain fruits*

皿の中の風景

水のほとりの四阿(あづまや)に　翁が琴を弾いてゐる
僮児(どうじ)は路を走ってゐる　雲の峰には鳥が二羽
霞の奥に帆が二つ　ああこの　皿の中の静かな風景
皿の外は春の宵　おほかた詩情を失った　憐れな詩人が夕餉を
　　する

山果集　*Sanka shū*

Scenery on a Plate

In a pavilion on a pond an old man strums his *koto*
A little boy runs down a path. Two birds fly past mountainous clouds
Two sails deep in the mist. Ah this quiet scenery on a plate
Beyond the plate is a spring evening. A pitiable poet, hardly any in-
   spiration left, eats his supper

1935. *Mountain fruits*

山鳩

山鳩が啼いてゐる‥‥
去年の春　この林を通った時も　やはり啼いてゐたつけな
鞍部（あんぶ）の小屋の煙出し　ああそれも　去年のままに傾（かし）
　　いでゐる
今日もまた　あそこまで登ってみよう　眸にしみる空の色

山果集　*Sanka shū*

Turtledove

A turtledove is calling ...
It was calling when I passed through this grove of trees last spring too
A chimney on a shack in the saddle of the hill—ah, that is also tilted
    just like last year
Today, too, I will climb up there. The blue of the sky dyes my eyes

1935. *Mountain fruits*

自畫像

　　　＊

ここに會した
翼ある空のルンペン

僕は無料宿泊所だ
天使がくる　梟がやってくる

僕は君らに切符をあげる
君らは眠るがいい

朝の子たち
夜の子たち

君らみな
空腹のハンモックに揺られて

　　　＊

太陽の下　水の上
煙の頸環を風にくれて

僕は川波を蹴って進む
僕はポンポン蒸気だ

二錢銅貨よりも古ぼけた
僕は一錢蒸気だ

人は橋に立って
僕を眺めて微笑する

Self-Portrait

*

Sky's winged vagrants
Meet here

I am rent-free lodging
Angels come. Owls arrive

I give you courtesy passes
Sleep here

Morning's children
Night's children

All of you
Swaying in hammocks of hunger

*

Under the sun, over the water
Giving the wind a necklace of smoke

I am a steamboat
Moving along beating the river waves

I am a steamboat a penny a ride
Older than a two-penny coin

People smile looking at me
As they stand on the bridge

輪を描いて
僕がしなをつくって見せるから

揺れる川波
寄る年波

けれども僕は快活だ
このエンジンはまだ廻る

その感情をすて給へ
橋下の僕を憐れむな

　　　　＊

蝶がくる
春の日に

一人の男が息絶える
いま身まかると知りながら

一つの詩が　こときれる
窓を見ながら

その窓に蝶がきて
舞ひ舞ふ　畫

霾　　*Tsuchifuru*

Because I move drawing a circle
Coquettishly showing off

The river waves sway
My years pile up

But I am happy
This engine of mine still revs

Throw away all your emotions
Do not pity me under the bridge

*

A butterfly visits
On a Spring day

A man takes his last breath
Knowing that is the moment of his passing

A piece of poetry expires
Looking at the window

To that window a butterfly comes
Twirling, dancing, in the mid-day

1939. *Dust devil*

涙

とある朝（あした）一つの花の花心から
昨夜（ゆうべ）の雨がこぼれるほど

小さきもの
小さきものよ

お前の眼から　お前の睫毛の間から
この朝（あした）　お前の小さな悲しみから

父の手に
こぼれて落ちる

今この父の手の上に　しばしの間温かい
ああこれは　これは何か

それは父の手を濡らし
それは父の心を濡らす

それは遠い國からの
それは遠い海からの

それはこのあはれな父の　その父の
そのまた父の　まぼろしの故郷（ふるさと）からの

鳥の歌と　花の匂ひと　青空と
はるかにつづいた山川との

――風のたより
なつかしい季節のたより

この朝（あした）この父の手に
新らしくとどいた消息

艸千里　*Kusasenri*

Tears

One morning, from the heart of a flower
Spills the last night's rain

Such a little one,
My dear little one,

From your eyes, from between your eyelashes
From your little sorrow this morning

It spills onto
Your father's palm

Now on your father's palm, it stays warm for a while
What is this?

It wets your father's hand
It soaks your father's heart

It is from a distant country
Across a distant sea

It is from the phantom homeland of your pitiable father
Of his father, of his father's father

It is a whisper of the wind
News of the season that brings back memories

Of songs of birds, scent of flowers, the blue sky
And of mountains and rivers that continue on far away

This morning your father received
A note fresh from you

1939. *Grassy crater basin*

あられふりける　二

ここにしてあふぎたまひし
まつがえにまつめとびかひ

ここにしていこひたまひし
かれくさはかれしままなる

あきはやくくれにけるかな
ふゆのひはとほくちひさく

うらやまのはざまのこみち
はらはらとあられふりける
　　　　　　あられふりける

艸千里　*Kusasenri*

Hail Comes Fluttering 2

You were here looking up
at the pine branches where pine-sparrows flit about

you were here resting on the withered grass
the grass remains, still withered

autumn has already come to an end
the winter sun seems so distant and small

on the trail in the valley of dark hills
softly hail comes fluttering
    hail comes fluttering

939. *Grassy crater basin*

桐の花

夢よりもふとはかなげに
桐の花枝をはなれて
ゆるやかに舞ひつつ落ちぬ
二つ三つ四つ
幸(さち)あるは風に吹かれて
おん肩にさやりて落ちぬ
色も香もたふとき花の
ねたましやその桐の花
晝ふかき土の上より
おん手の上にひろはれぬ

艸千里　*Kusasenri*

Paulownia Flowers

More ephemeral than a dream
Paulownia flowers leave their branches
Flutter down slowly dancing
Two, three, four
Lucky ones ride on the wind
Touch your shoulders and fall
Noble in color and scent
I envy those paulownia flowers
Your hand lifts
From the earth at mid-day

1939. *Grassy crater basin*

家庭

息子が學校へ上るので
親父は毎日詩(うた)を書いた
詩は帽子やランドセルや
教科書やクレイヨンや
小さな蝙蝠傘になった
四月一日
櫻の花の咲く町を
息子は母親につれられて
古いお城の中にある
国民學校第一年の
入學式に出かけていった
静かになった家の中で
親父は年とつた女中と二人
久しぶりできくやうに
鶉どりのなくのをきいてゐた
海の鳴るのをきいてゐた

一点鐘　*Ittenshō*

Family

As his son was to start school
Dad wrote songs everyday
The songs turned into a cap, a satchel
textbooks, crayons
and a small umbrella
On the first day of April
his son went with Mom
through the town full of cherry blossoms
to the People's School in an old castle
to attend its first grade entrance ceremony
At home, now left quiet,
Dad was alone with an aged maid
listening to bulbuls' calls
listening to the sea's roar
as if he hadn't heard them for a long time

1941. *Striking one o'clock*

毀れた窓

廢屋のこはれた窓から
五月の海が見えてゐる

硝子のない硝子戸越しに
そいつが素的なまつ晝間だ

波は一日ながれてゐるその額縁に
ポンポン船がやってくる

灰色の鷗もそこに集って
何かしばらく解けない謎を解いてゐる

あとはまたなんにもない青い海だが
それがまた何とも妙に心にしみる

ぽっかり一つそんな時鯨がそこに浮いたつて
よささうな鹽梅風にも見えるのだ

それをぼんやり見てゐるとどういふものか
俺の眼にはふと故郷の街がうかんできた

古い石造建築のどうやら銀行らしいやつの
くつきりとした日かげを俺が歩いてゐる

まだ二十前の俺がそれから廣場をまた突切つてゆくのだ
ああそれらの日ももうかへつては來なくなった……

Broken Window

Through the broken window of a deserted house
I see the ocean in May

Through the missing glass
At mid-day the ocean is lovely

Within that picture frame where waves move all day
A steamboat appears

Gray gulls gather there too
Trying to solve unsolvable puzzles for a while

The plain blue ocean is left alone again, but
Somehow it feels close to my heart

It would look all right
If a whale popped up there at a time like this

As I gaze, somehow
Streets of my hometown appear in front of my eyes

I am walking in the clearly defined shadow
Of an old stone building that looks like a bank

I then cross the town square—I am not yet twenty—
Ah those days will never return …

そんな思出でもない思出が
隨分しばらく俺の眼さきに浮んでゐた

どういふ仕掛けの窓だらう
何しろこいつは素的な窓だ

丘の上の
松の間の

廢屋のこはれた窓から
五月の海が見えてゐる

一点鐘　*Ittenshō*

Those memories, not particularly memorable,
Float in my vision for quite a while

This window, what tricks does it know?
Whatever, it's a lovely window

On the hill
Among pine trees

Is a deserted house, and from its broken window
I see the ocean in May

1941. *Striking one o'clock*

謎の音樂

春の日のうすら黄ばんだ沙の上に
日もすがらしづかに囁いてゐる海

どこまでも遠くはるかにひろがつた
このはてしない青い海原

海とは何だらう
そもそもこの眺望は

小さな船を七つ八つ
今しも遠くへつれてゆく

海よ
こころよい不可思議

解きがたい謎の
音楽

一点鐘　*Ittenshō*

MYSTERIOUS MUSIC

On faintly yellowed sands under the Spring sun
The sea quietly whispers all day long

This endless blue seascape
stretching far far away

What does this sea mean?
What is this spectacle to start with?

You are now taking
seven or eight small ships far away

Dear Sea,
You are a pleasant wonder

Unresolvable mystery of
Music

1941. *Striking one o'clock*

ことのねたつな

いとけなきなれがをゆびに
かいならすねはつたなけれ
そらにみつやまとことうた
ひとふしのしらべはさやけ
つまづきつとだえつするを
おいらくのちちはききつつ
いはれなきなみだをおぼゆ
かかるひのあさなあさなや
もののふはよものいくさを
たたかはすときとはいへど
そらにみつやまとのくにに
をとめらのことのねたつな

寒柝　*Kantaku*

May the *Koto*'s Resonance Soar

Artless are the notes
your childlike fingers strum
the *koto* music of Japan soars to the sky
listening to you play a melody
clean, then tripping, and halting
your aging father tears up with no cause
even though the times are such that
warriors are fighting many battles
morning after morning like this day
may maidens' *koto* melodies resonate
soaring to the sky overarching our nation

1943. *Wooden clappers in the cold*

わが名をよびて

わが名をよびてたまはれ
いとけなき日のよび名もてわが名をよびてたまはれ
あはれいまひとたびわがいとけなき日の名をよびてたまはれ
風のふく日のとほくよりわが名をよびてたまはれ
庭のかたへに茶の花のさきのこる日の
ちらちらと雪のふる日のとほくよりわが名をよびてたまはれ
よびてたまはれ
わが名をよびてたまはれ

花筺　*Hanagatami*

CALL MY NAME

Call my name please
call me by my childhood name please
pity me and call me just once more by my childhood name
call my name from the distant day when the wind was blowing, please
call me please from the distant day when snowflakes were lightly
    dancing
when the tea bush still held a few blossoms in the corner of our yard
call me please
call my name please

1944. *Flower basket*

我ら戰爭に敗れたあとに

我ら戰爭に敗れたあとに
一千萬人の赤んぼが生れた

だから海はまつ青で
空はだからまつ青だ

見たまへ血のやうな
ぽっちりと赤い太陽

骨甕へ骨甕へ　骨甕へ
齢とつた二十世紀の半分は

何も彼もやり直しだと跛（びっこ）の蟀（こほろぎ）
葉の落ちつくした森の奥

まどかな丘のひとうねり
冬の畑の豆の花

歴史は何をしるしたか
雲が來てすべてをぬぐふ

まつ青な空
まつ青な海

After We Were Defeated at War

After we were defeated at war
ten million babies were born

That is why the sea is deep blue
the sky is, therefore, deep blue

Look, like a drop of blood
the sun is a red dot

To crematory urns, to crematory urns, to crematory urns
marched a half of the aging twentieth century

Crippled crickets say they'll start all over from scratch
in the depths of woods where the leaves have all fallen

A gentle rolling expanse
bean plants flower in a winter field

What did history record?
clouds come and wipe it all away

The deep blue sky
the deep blue sea

飛行機はあそこに墜ち
軍艦はあそこへ沈んだ

萬葉集の歌のとなりに
砲彈の唸りをきくのは

まばらに伐られた林の奥に
それは何ものの影であらうか

けれどもまつ青な
空と海

我ら戰争に敗れたあとに
一千萬人の赤んぼが生れた

故郷の花　*Kokyō no hana*

Planes fell over there
warships sank out there

To hear the roar of artillery shells
next to ancient poetry of *Man'yo shū*—

What is casting shadows
in the depths of woods randomly deforested?

Yet the sky and the sea are
deep blue

After we were defeated at war
ten million babies were born

1946. *Flowers from home*

胡桃讃

　——季刊詩誌「胡桃」創刊號のために

外殻堅けれども
指頭に轉ずれば聲あり
聲はかすかにして笑ふが如し
面白きかな胡桃
内に滋味を藏す
詩も亦かくの如くにして佳し
栗鼠よくこれを解し
雙手に禮拜す
拜して食(を)し
食し了って一閃
去って電光と化す

砂の砦　*Suna no toride*

In Praise of the Walnut

For the inaugural issue of the poetry quarterly *Kurumi* (Walnut)

Its shell is tough, yet
As I roll it in my fingertips I hear a voice
The voice is faint, and seems to laugh
How fascinating the walnut is
It holds richness within
So does poetry when it is fine
A squirrel knows this well
He puts two hands together and worships
He prays and eats
As he's done with eating—a flash
He's gone, turning into lightning

1946. *Fort of sand*

村酒雑詠

日もくれぬ

日も暮れぬ己(し)が盞を
みたせただ餘はそらごとぞ
己が詩(うた)をみづからうたへ
月やがて松にかからん

盞は

盞はちひさけれども
ただたのむ夕べの友ぞ
おほかたはひとをたばかる
世にありてせんすべしらに

死後の名は

死後の名はとにもあるべし
一盞の酒にもしかず
わが師かくのらしたまひぬ
われは師の言にしたがふ

駱駝の瘤にまたがって　Rakuda no kobu ni matagatte

Verses on a Village Brew

The Day Has Ended

The day has ended. Fill your
Own saké-cup, the rest is all in vain
Sing to yourself your own verse
The moon will soon hang on the pines

The Saké-cup

The saké-cup is small, yet
In a world where many are deceitful
I trust only this companion of my evening
I know no other way

A Posthumous Name

A posthumous name can be whatever
It won't amount to a small cup of saké
So pronounced my master
I heed my master's words

1952. *Straddling the camel's hump*

なつかしい斜面

なつかしい斜面だ
おれはこんな枯草の斜面にひとりで坐つてゐるのが好きだ
電車の音を遠くききながら
さみしいいぢけた冬の雲でも眺めてゐよう
ああ遠くおれの運んできたいつさいのもの思ひ
疲れたやくざなおれの希望なら　そこらの枯草にはふり出してしまへ
かうして疲れた貧しい男が疲れた貧しい心をいたはつてゐるのは
何といふあてどのないおだやかな幸福だらう
けれどもおれの病気の心は　それでもまだ知らない世界を考へてゐる
無限に遠く　夢のやうに遠くどこかへひろがつてゆかうとする
意志を感ずる
意志を感ずる
ああその意志を不幸な轅（ながえ）から解き放してやれ　そいつは愚かな驢馬なんだよ
病気の愚かな驢馬なんだから向ふの方の松の木にでも繋いでやれ
彼をしてしづかに彼の夢を見しめよ……
晝間もぐつすり寝こんでゐる
そいつの向ふを遠まはりして
電車の音はあとからあとから忙がしい都會の人口を運んでゐるが
まつ晝間だつて何だつてぐつすり寝こんでゐる奴がゐるものだ

This Slope Brings Back Memories

This slope brings back memories
I like sitting alone on a slope of dry grass like this
I hear trains in the distance
I will stay gazing at the perverse lonely clouds of winter
Bearing the load of a heavy heart I have traveled from afar
This tired and worthless hope of mine, cast it away into the dry weeds over here
What aimless placid happiness it is
For a destitute and drained man to console his impoverished and weary heart
But my ailing heart still broods over a yet unknown world
Aiming to span an eternal distance like a dream to reach somewhere far
I sense my will
I sense my will
Ah release the will from his luckless harness. He's a stupid ass, you see
Because he's a sick stupid ass, just tie him to a pine tree over there
Let him quietly dream his own dreams …
And leave him alone to eat the surrounding yellowed dry grass as he pleases
At the far bottom of this slope is a pool of putrid city water, and the dim geometric moat is
Sound asleep even during the day
Skirting around the longer edge of the moat
The sound of one train after another moves through the busy urban population, yet
There are those who are deeply asleep, even at high noon or any other time

おれにしたつてさうかもしれぬ　さうだらう
そんなことならおれにしたつてもうとつくの昔に悟ってゐることだ
このぼろ船はいつになつたつて港につかぬ
港は遠く見失はれて　波は高く　海は廣い
機關はやぶれて燃料はつきてしまったのだ
かまはず積荷をはふり投げて
こいつはかうしてここまでどうやらやつて来たのだ
焼け野つ原の都會の空をいぢけた雲が飛んでゐる
愚かな驢馬は向ふの方で
それでもあいつの性分だから　耳だけひくひくやつてゐる
すてておけ　仕方もないことだ

駱駝の瘤にまたがって　*Rakuda no kobu ni matagatte*

Isn't this true of me, too?
I came to realize something of the sort a long time ago
This rickety boat will never even reach port
The harbor is lost in the distance; the waves are high and the sea is vast
The engine is broken and out of fuel
Recklessly throwing its cargo overboard
It has managed to come this far
Perverse clouds fly in the sky above the city burned to the ground
That stupid ass is over there
Pricking up his ears as he was born to do
Let him be, there's nothing we can do about it

1952. *Straddling the camel's hump*

けれども情緒は

けれども情緒は春のやうだ
一人の老人がかう呟いた
焼け野つ原の砌の上で
孤獨な膝をだいてゐる一つの運命がさう呟いた
妻もなく家庭もなく隣人もなく
名譽も希望も職業も　歸るべき故郷もなく
貧しい襤褸（らんる）につつまれて　語られ終つたわびしい一つの物語り
谿間をへだてた向ふから呼びかへしてくる谺のやうな　老人がさう呟いた
かひがひしい妻　やさしい家族　暮しなれた習慣と隣人と
そのささやかな幸福のすべてがかつてそこにあった
焼け野つ原の砌（みぎり）の上で
薄暮の雨に消えてゆく直線圖形の堀割のむかふの方
みづがね色の遠景に畸型に歪んでおびえてゐる戰災ビルの肩を越えて
病気の貧しい子供らが歌ひはじめる唱歌のこゑ——
それはまばらにさむざむと　またたのしげに　瞬きはじめた都会の灯（ひ）
ああその薔薇いろの瞳とほく輝きはじめた眼くばせが
しかしいま私に何のかかはりがあらう
そのまたずつとむかふの空に重たく暗く沈んでゆく山脈に
けふの私の一日が遮ぎり断たれ　つひには虚無にしまひこまれて消えてゆく黄昏時に
いつまでもいつまでも
空しく風にゆれてゐる柳のかげをたち去らぬこのおだやかなこのつかれた　この孤獨な情緒は　情緒はまるで春のやうだ……
一人の老人が額をふせてさう呟いた

Yet, a Stirring in Me Seems

Yet, a stirring in me seems like Spring,
mutters an old man to himself
so mutters fate as it holds its own lonesome knees
on a flat stone in a burnt-over field
so mutters the old man like an echo calling back from across
    the valley
a sad life's tale that has come to an end, wrapped in indigent tatters,
with no wife, no family, no neighbors,
no fame, no hope, no work, no homeland to return to
once he had an agile wife, gentle family, homey habits and neighbors
he possessed such modest yet wholesome happiness
on a flat stone in the burnt field
over the shoulders of bombed-out buildings, disfigured
and frightened against the mercury-tinted background
far beyond geometric canals disappearing into the twilight rain
he hears children's songs as poor sick kids begin to sing—
their voices, scattered, cold, yet happy, are city lights beginning to
    blink
ah, those rose-colored eyes begin to shine in the distance, winking,
but what have they to do with me now?
sinking heavy and dark against the sky farther out
the mountain ridges block out and shut down this day of my life
to finally fold it into nothingness in the dusk
this gentle listlessness refusing to leave from under a willow idly
    swaying in the wind
lingering for a long long time
this solitary feeling, this stirring is like Spring … mutters the lone old
    man to himself with his head lowered,

けれども情緒は　情緒はまるで春のやうだ
しのしのとのび放題に生ひ繁った草つ原
──その枯れ枯れにうら枯れはてたそこらあたりに
おもたく澱んだ堀割の水がくされてゐる
そこいらいちめん崩れかかった煉瓦塀の間から　雀の群れが飛
　　びたつた
気まぐれな思出のやうに　一つ一つ弱い翼を羽ばたいて
巷の小鳥も飛び去ってゆく夕暮れだ
霧のやうに降つてくるしめつぽい冬の雨の中で
けれども情緒は　情緒はいまこの男に
朧ろにかすんだ遠い日の櫻日和を思はせた
遠い沙漠の砂の上でひもじく飢ゑて死んでゆく蝗のやうな感情に
とぼしい光の落ちかかるうすぼんやりした内景から聴き手もなく
　　老人はひとり呟いた
けれども情緒は　情緒はまるで春のやうだ

駱駝の瘤にまたがって　*Rakuda no kobu ni matagatte*

yet the stirring is, the stirring feels like Spring
the field is wildly overgrown with weeds
—the field all around is now withered and in distress
the canal water is putrid, heavy and stagnant
a flock of sparrows takes flight from bricks scattered about crumbling
    walls
it is evening when every small bird in town,
like a whimsical memory, beats its feeble wings to take off
in a gloomy wintry rain falling like a mist
yet the stirring … the stirring has brought this man a memory of
    some distant past
of a hazy spring day with cherry blossoms in full bloom
out of his obscure mindscape where scant light illuminates his feel-
    ings like
a locust dying of hunger in the sands of a distant desert,
the old man mumbles to himself, with no one around to hear him,
yet this stirring in me, this stirring feels just like Spring

1952. *Straddling the camel's hump*

空のなぎさ

いづこよ遠く來りし旅人は
冬枯れし梢のもとにいこひたり
空のなぎさにさしかはす
梢のすゑはしなめきて
煙らひしなひさやさやにささやくこゑす
仰ぎ見つかつはきく遠き音づれ
落葉つみ落葉はつみて
あたたかき日ざしのうへに
はやここに角(つの)ぐむものはむきむきに
おのがじし彼らが堅き包みものときほどくなる
路のくま樹下石上に晝の風歩みとどまり
旅人なればおのづから組みし小指にまつはりぬ
かくありて今日のゆくてをささんとす小指のすゑに

百たびののち　Hyakutabi no nochi

The Shore of the Sky

Where are you from, traveler from afar,
Resting in treetops bared by the winter?
The treetops are lithe
In the haze, arching, rustling, whispering
Crossing their swords on the shore of the sky
I look up and hear their distant sounds
Dry leaves are piled on fallen leaves
In the warm sunlight
Hard buds have already formed
But those tight packages will unfold on their own
The midday wind pauses at the deep ends of alleys, under trees, over stones
Being a traveler it coils around my clasped fingers
Poised thus on the tips of my fingers it points to today's journey

1962. *After one hundred times*

NAGASE KIYOKO
永瀬清子

Nagase Kiyoko
(1906–1995)

LIFE AND CAREER

As a poet and a woman Nagase Kiyoko was a quiet revolutionary, both in her private life and in her poetry. At the age of eighteen she decided to be a poet after reading New Style poetry, and approached a brilliant young poet, Satō Sōnosuke, to be her "teacher." She committed herself to poetry from that point on, producing powerful work to the end of her career, even while working a farm in the postwar period to support her family. In everything she did she was sustained by an unshakeable belief in the value, strength, and resilience of women. It was a radical idea for her time, but to her it was a fundamental truth. She proclaimed it in her writing and later in life put it in practice as an outspoken activist in antinuclear, antiwar, and feminist movements in Japan's postwar period.

Born during Japan's ascent to the status of a world power, Nagase could not help but observe that while the country was undergoing sweeping changes in many aspects of society, women were still subject to men, and had virtually no rights of their own. A popular saying held that "a woman must be obedient to men—first her father, then her husband, and finally her son." This was the formula for preserving family unity under the prevailing Confucian moral code. Nagase, however, though a wife, mother, and working woman, always insisted on living on her own terms and maintaining her devotion to her art.

There was precedence for her attitude: she was rooted in the Okayama region, which was the birthplace of the Japanese women's movement, as she writes in *Nagase Kiyoko shishū* (Poems of Nagase Kiyoko):

In 1882 a women's conference, which was rare in Japan, was founded in Okayama. The wives and sisters of those men who were active in the movement for civic rights and freedom in the 1880s realized that women, who had been subordinated to their men and families, needed to become aware of their issues, and called to women and organized speeches and established schools. They were the pioneers in Japan.[1]

She goes on to note that 1882 was also the year when *Shintaishi shō* (Selection of New Style poetry) was published, marking the beginning of modern poetry in Japan. For her the birth of modern poetry aligns with the coming dawn of an improved status for women.

In spite of her convictions, her poetry is neither polemical nor didactic. While trust in herself, womanhood, and motherhood formed the core of her writing throughout her hard-working life, her poetry is not framed in terms of the politics of women's rights. Instead, she uses her remarkable powers of observation to distill the realities of life into poetry that is both highly personal and strikingly universal.

Nagase was born in Okayama Prefecture in 1906, while her father was studying at Kyoto Imperial University. He completed his education as an electrical engineer, found a job in Kanazawa, and moved there with his family when she was two. As the only child of a highly intellectual father she received a superb education, starting kindergarten at age three. In 1924 the family moved to Nagoya in Aichi Prefecture, where she was admitted to Aichi Prefectural First Women's School of Higher Education, majoring in English. That year she read a collection of poems by Ueda Bin[2] and was so inspired by his writing that she wanted to be a poet. She sent her poems to the brilliant young poet Satō Sōnosuke and became a member of his coterie group, which published the magazine *Shi no ie* (House of poetry). Both Murō Saisei and Kaneko Mitsuharu recognized Satō as "a young star of hope in

---

1. Nagase Kiyoko, *Nagase Kiyoko shishū* (Poems of Nagase Kiyoko) (Tokyo: Shichōsha, 1979), 128.

2. Ueda Bin (1874–1916) was a poet, translator, and literary critic. He introduced symbolism to Japan. His book of European and English poetry in translation, *Kaichō on* (Sound of the tide) published in 1905, is renowned for the artistry and elegance of the translated verse. The book influenced many contemporary and later poets.

1920 and thereabouts,"[3] as Kaneko put it. Nagase received practical advice and stylistic instruction on writing modern poetry from Satō, which Nagase took to heart and practiced throughout her career. Satō remained her mentor until his death in 1942.

Nagase graduated from the Women's School of Higher Education in 1927. Because she was a woman she was not allowed to pursue further education, so she agreed to marry the young man her parents had chosen, provided that he promise to let her continue to write poetry. At a time when a wife's duty was to serve her husband and manage household matters such a premarital agreement was extremely unusual, if not unthinkable. Remarkably, her husband kept his word, and respected poetry writing as her sanctuary throughout their long marriage.[4] For her part, her poems sometimes reveal a sense of guilt for not being an ordinary wife.

She published her first book of poems, *Gurenderu no hahaoya* (Grendel's mother), in 1930. As the title poem powerfully demonstrates, the strength of women and the power of motherhood were already prominent in her writing. She moved to Tokyo when her husband was transferred there the next year, and joined several coterie magazine groups in the city. *Shokoku no ten'nyo* (Heavenly maidens on earth), her second collection, was published in 1940. During the war she moved back to Okayama prefecture with her husband, but he was drafted into the military so she lived with her mother. When her husband returned at the end of the war they moved into her parents' old house. In order to support the family she took up farming for the first time in her life on a plot of family land. During the day she worked all by herself in the rice paddies. She would then sleep for a few hours, and afterward arise to write poetry until dawn. She continued this regimen for nearly twenty years, until her husband retired from his position in an insurance company in 1955 and joined her to work the farm.

---

3. Kaneko, *Poet*, 112.

4. Ikubo Itoko, *Josei shi no naka no Nagase Kiyoko–sengo hen* (Nagase Kiyoko in the course of women's history: postwar period) (Tokyo: Domesushuppan, 2009), 444.

When the end of World War II brought a democratic constitution recognizing women's rights, Nagase welcomed the change and expanded the range of her activities, both literary and social. Her reputation as a poet was on the rise, and she joined the Japan Futurist Group coterie magazine in 1947. She published *Ōinaru jumoku* (A great big tree) the same year, and *Utsukushii kuni* (Beautiful country) in 1948. In 1949 she was named the first recipient of the Okayama Prefecture Cultural Award, and in 1952 she and six other women poets founded a coterie magazine for women poets called *Ki bara* (Yellow roses), whose title symbolized the women of the region. Nagase personally edited 123 issues of the magazine through 1987.

In 1963 she became a "working woman" for the first time in her life, taking a job at the World Federation secretariat of the Okayama Prefectural Office. She chaired a local women's association, and represented it at the Conference of Asian Countries in New Delhi. In the postwar democratic environment new conferences were organized to promote causes that included peace, motherhood, and women's rights, and she chose to attend most of those conferences. She was a founding member and chair of the Study Group on Women's History in Okayama, established in 1982.

Nagase wrote prolifically throughout this period of increased activity and into her late years, her poetry retaining its freshness until the end. Her consistently straightforward, powerful diction and rhythm won her recognition from the Japan Poets' Association as a Pioneer Poet in 1982. *Akegata ni kuru hito yo* (To you who come at dawn), published in 1987, was awarded the Earth Prize for that year, followed by the *Misesu* (Mrs.) Modern Women Poets Prize in 1988. She was invited to the Imperial Palace to meet Empress Michiko, who had been moved by her work at her poetry reading; the Empress's invitation was repeated the following summer. The Empress's own English translation of the book's title poem was published in Japan PEN Club's Modern Japanese Literature #13 in 1988. Nagase published a total of twelve books of poetry (the last of which appeared two months after her death in 1995), six books of selected poems, four books of aphorisms, and five collections of her prose works.

POETRY

Motherhood, love, yearning for freedom, and whole-hearted devotion to poetry are key themes in Nagase's poetry. She was not blind to the frailty of women, as evident in "You in the Shade of a Tree," but feminine strength is her central concern. "Grendel's Mother," the title poem of her first book, embodies her trust in the power and resilience of motherhood and love. The poem is about the mother of the water monster in the ancient tale of Beowulf; feminine strength is clearly Nagase's theme. She also creates a temporal structure that melds ancient myth with modern reality, using parenthetical asides to insert scenery from modern times into her narrative: "(or at the bottom of a gloomy city / where electric poles cast shadows)." This technique communicates her insight that the feminine spirit, exemplified by Grendel's mother, transcends time and space. Considering that Nagase lived in a society where women were expected to be totally subservient to men, it is startling to see her focus so forcefully on the power and dignity of women. It is no less remarkable that she came up with a highly original way to present this advanced idea as a timeless truth. The poem's structural innovation, verbal clarity, and modern theme make it seem current and timeless, eighty years after she wrote it.

Timelessness is one of the outstanding qualities of Nagase's poetry. Her work is not bound by the period in which it is written, nor by its original inspiration. Her voice may be impassioned, but it is never restricted by the personal or emotional impulse behind it. In "Song of a Woman," for example, the speaker is angered by her demanding and unappreciative husband. The reader can hear and feel her frustration and pain, but as her imagination releases her from earthly realities, her emotions in that specific situation are transmuted into the universal concerns of all women, and the voice achieves an omniscient character.

The images in Nagase's poetry are definitely grounded in real-world objects such as trees, flames, or a vortex, but they lead to a deeper level of consciousness when seen through her analytical mind's eye. The reader no longer experiences these images as specific to Nagase's own self. In one of her aphorisms, "In the Same Manner," she explains:

> In the same manner I keep querying about the mind's construct. That is my job. Poetry is written in order to gain insight into what I really am, a small minute being in this universe.
> Nothing else is significant.
> Because the self is a small magnifier, and also a glass globe, there is no choice but to look through it.[5]

Throughout her long career Nagase maintained her own consistent poetic voice in a style that is elegant yet down to earth, straightforward, clear, and evocative. She credits her mentor's advice for her focus and consistency.

> It was in the twelfth year of the Taishō Era [1923] [sic] when I thought I wanted to be a poet. That was the year I first read *Poems of Ueda Bin*, and also the year I sent my poems to my master, Mr. Satō Sōnosuke. Of course I could not possibly write poetry in the manner Ueda Bin did in his translations (I was eighteen then) and, besides, my master told me, "Forget all poetic diction of the past. Observe with your own eyes."
> I was given by him the fundamental premise for facing poetry. ... [His words] were carved into me as the supreme command. And when I showed him a poem I titled "Melancholy by the Seashore," he scolded me by saying "Melancholy is passé ... others have written about it. Write your heart with words of your own." I received enlightenment at that moment.[6]

The power of this enlightenment sustained her through a career that spanned most of the twentieth century. She wrote "her heart," singularly and relentlessly focusing on her perceptions, thoughts, and imaginations. "Her heart" was open to all aspects of experience. In "You in the Shade of a Tree," we meet a woman whose heart is con-

---

5. Nagase Kiyoko, *Tanshō shū* (Aphorisms) (Tokyo: Shichōsha, 2007), 24.
6. Nagase Kiyoko, *Nagase Kiyoko* (Tokyo: Shichōsha, 1990), 125.

flicted at an elegant outdoor gathering reminiscent of an Impressionist painting. The woman is speaking with a distinguished man. She is proud of standing on her own, but also keenly conscious of his lovely blue-eyed wife's concerned gaze. While the woman insists that her motive for speaking with the man is purely intellectual, she also knows that like any other woman she has dressed to enhance her own femininity. In this poem Nagase dramatizes the duality of a woman's heart. It is also a telling example of her unflinching honesty about herself, her subject matter, and her poetry. There is no superficial romanticizing, fantasizing, or dreaming. Her poetic world is a construct generated from her heart, forever pursuing poetry. Her constant concern was to renew and rekindle herself:

> [The poet] cannot be a true genius
> without constantly adding something that hasn't been poetry before
> just like we add firewood to maintain flames.[7]

At eighty-one years of age she published *Akegata ni kuru hito yo* (To you who come at dawn). Its title poem is an aged woman's recollection of her disappointed attempt to elope with her love. Her trembling heart and overwhelming anxiety are still painfully alive; she continues to wait for this love to appear. We realize this is not just a human love. It is also her art. She is presenting a tale of the pursuit of poetry by a woman who has never lost the attributes of an innocent yet unflinching young girl.

Another of the poems in this book, "My Dear Silent One, My Indigo Mist," is a touching dirge for her husband who passed away suddenly in 1984. It conveys raw pain about her loss, but her sorrow blends into an indigo mist, as if to embrace us all in our individual experiences of loss. Thus the poem refines elements from her life into universal truth. That is the hallmark of Nagase's art throughout her six-decade career.

---

7. Nagase Kiyoko, *Tanshō shū zoku* (Aphorisms II) (Tokyo: Shichōsha, 2008), 63.

グレンデルの母親は

グレンデルの母親は
青い沼の果の
その古代の洞窟の奥に
　（或は又電柱の翳のさす
　冥い都会の底に）
銅色の髪でもつて
子供たちをしつかりと抱いてゐる

古怪なるその瞳で
蜘蛛のやうに入口を凝視してゐる
逞ましいその母性で
兜のやうに護つてゐる

子供たちはやがて
北方の大怪となるだらう
　（或は幾多の人々の涙を
　無言でしつかり飲みほす者となるだらう）

悽愴たる犠牲者の中をも
孤りでサブライムの方へ歩んでゆくだらう
悪と憤怒の中にも熔けないだらう
そして母親の腕の中以外には
悲鳴の咆哮をもらさぬだらう！

新鮮な礦物のやうな
夜の潭（ふか）みからのぼる月の光は
古代の沼に
（或は都会の屋根瓦に）
青く燃え立ち
グレンデルの母親は
今洞窟の奥にひそんでゐる

グレンデルの母親　　*Grendel no hahaoya*

Grendel's Mother

In the depths of her ancient cavern
at the far edge of a cyan marsh
    (or at the bottom of a gloomy city
    where electric poles cast shadows)
Grendel's Mother
with her bronze hair
holds her children tightly in her arms

Her ancient monster's eyes
watch the entrance like a spider's
her powerful motherhood like a helmet
gives them protection

Her children will become
great monsters of the North in due time
    (or they will grow up to
    steadily lap up the tears of multitudes in silence)

Each, alone, will step toward the sublime
even among their gruesome victims
will not melt away even amid evil and wrath
and will not roar in pain
except in Mother's arms!

Moonlight like fresh ore
rises from the profound depths of night
flares in cyan
over the ancient marsh
(or over the roof tiles in the city)
Grendel's Mother
is now hiding in the depths of the cavern.

1930. *Grendel's mother*

諸国の天女

諸国の天女は漁夫や猟人を夫として
いつも忘れ得ず想ってゐる、
底なき天を翔けた日を。

人の世のたつきのあはれないとなみ
やすむひまなきあした夕べに
わが忘れぬ喜びを人は知らない。
井の水を汲めばその中に
天の光がしたたつてゐる
花咲けば花の中に
かの日の天の着物がそよぐ。
雨と風とがささやくあこがれ
我が子に唄へばそらんじて
何を意味するとか思ふのだろう。

せめてぬるめる春の波間に
或る日はかづきつ嘆かへば
涙はからき潮にまじり
空ははるかに金のひかり

ああ遠い山々を過ぎゆく雲に
わが分身の乗りゆく姿
さあれかの水蒸気みどりの方へ
いつの日か去る日もあらば
いかに嘆かんわが人々は

きづなは地にあこがれは空に
うつくしい樹木にみちた岸辺や谷間で
いつか年月のまにまに
冬過ぎ春来て諸国の天女も老いる。

　　*かづく=水にもぐる

諸国の天女　　Shokoku no tennyo

Heavenly Maidens on Earth

Heavenly maidens on earth, wedded to fishermen and hunters,
always long for, unable to forget,
the days when we flew freely through the boundless heavens.

No one knows the joy I cannot forget
while life's doleful grind of making a living
goes on from morning to evening with no respite.
As I draw water from the well
the heavenly light shimmers in it;
as flowers bloom
the heavenly robe of my past billows in them.
I sing to my own children
of my yearning, whispered in the rain and wind
they learn it by heart
they may wonder what it means.

One day to console myself
I take a dip in ocean waves warmed by the Spring
my tears mix with the salty sea
the sky is far away, shining gold

Ah, part of me rides on a cloud
passing over distant ridges
Yet if I should someday leave
for that vapor-green
how my family will lament

Bound to the earth, while longing for the sky
on shores and in valleys filled with glorious trees
as the years drift on with winters passing, springs arriving
heavenly maidens on earth also grow old.

1940. *Heavenly maidens on earth*

大いなる樹木

我は大いなる樹木とならん
そのみどり濃き円錐の静もりて
宿れるものを窺い得ざるまで。
素足を水に垂るるごと
人知れぬ地下の流れを
わが根の汲めるよろこびにまで。

我は大いなる樹木とならん
われを見る人おのずから
安息(やすらぎ)の念(おもい)をおぼゆるまで。

されどわがしげき枝と葉の
おくれ毛のごとく微風にも応えん
誰よりもさとく薔薇なす朝の光に先づ覚めん
地にしるす青き翳の
レエスの裳のごとくひろがりて
われが想いのやさしからん
われが想いのすずしからん
樹は行かず
樹は云わず
されど天の子供の降り且昇る梯子ならん

まひるわがもとに立寄り憩うものあらば
われふかき翳と尽きざる慰めとを与えん

A Great Big Tree

May I be a great big tree
A deep green conical figure wrapped in serenity
So tall that I can't see those taking shelter under me
May my roots joyfully draw
From an unknown subterranean current
Just as I dangle my bare feet in the water

May I be a great big tree
So that those who look at me
Will naturally feel peace and repose

Yet may my luxuriating branches and leaves
Whisper to a breeze like stray hair
May they awaken before anyone else in the rosy glow of mornings
May their blue shadows be cast on earth
spreading like a trailing lace skirt
May my thoughts be kind
May my thoughts be refreshing
The tree will not move
The tree will not speak
Yet may it be a ladder heavenly children ascend and descend

If someone comes and rests by me at the height of day
I will provide deep shadow and infinite comfort

嵐の日
更に我は大いならん勁からん
根は大地をふみてゆるぎなからん
されど樹液の流れみだるるなく
瘡痍さえすずしき匂いをはなち
やがて又ほほえみの唄をささやかん
夜来りなは闇に溶け去りて
人知れぬ時に
その唄のみは見えざるさざなみとならん

大いなる樹木　Ōinaru jumoku

On a stormy day
May I be even greater, more stalwart
May I firmly anchor my roots in the great earth and not sway
Yet may my sap flow smoothly
May my incised wounds even issue forth a refreshing scent
Soon I will whisper a smiling song
When night arrives I will dissolve away into darkness
Unbeknownst to people
May my song alone become invisible ripples

1947. *A great big tree*

早春

あけ方にふと目がさめると
空気がなんとなくにぎやかだ。
春が来ている。
地虫や草の芽のよろこびが
気温の中にこもっている。
私の心もしずかにもどけて
生れてから過したたくさんの春の
やさしいとりどりの思い出がよみがえつて来る。
早く死んだ昔の人が
世にくたびれた私にいたわりの声をかけてくれる。
しずかにあけてゆく空色の中に
オレンジジュースがそそがれる。
その時自分に対してもきびしすぎたことが
やつと私にわかつてくる。
ああかの人にばかりでなく——。
すっかり朝があけると
古い径に欅のこまかい枝の影が
まるで焔のようにあおくきらめく。

大いなる樹木　Ōinaru jumoku

Early Spring

At daybreak I suddenly awaken.
The air is somehow full of energy.
Spring is here.
Grubs and grass shoots
infuse their joy into the warm air.
My heart also quietly dissolves
and recalls gentle colorful memories
of many springs I have lived since I was born.
Someone from long ago, who died young,
calls out to console me, grown tired of this world.
Into the sky-blue, slowly spreading,
orange juice is being poured.
Then, it comes to me
that I have been too hard on myself as well,
ah, not only on him—.
When the day breaks completely
shadows of the delicate branches of a zelkova tree
flicker like blue flames over the familiar path.

1947. *A great big tree*

そよ風のふく日に

　　○

そよ風の吹く日にお前は来た
突然天からころげ落ちたように泣きながら
お前のために何でも堪え忍ぶよと云う叫びが
牝獅子やなんがが思うように
その時突然私の中におこつた。

　　○

まだ目もよく見えないのに
天の仲間を思いだしている赤ん坊
誰も乗っていないぶらんこが
かすかに風にゆれているように
朝の光の中でやさしい笑い顔をしている。

　　○

暑い日がはじまるようだ。
窓の竹の葉に黄金(きん)色の露の玉がのぼつている
一日一日回復してゆく私。
働ける日の幸福を待ちながら
しばらく憩う時間のきれいな水たまり。

On a Day with a Gentle Breeze

*

You arrived on a day with a gentle breeze
crying suddenly as if rolling out of heaven
all of a sudden, in that instant, inside me
rose the roar of a lioness,
"I will endure anything for you!"

*

A baby recalling its heavenly friends
though its eyes still do not see well
smiles gently in the morning light
the way an empty swing
sways slightly in the breeze.

*

It looks like the start of a hot day.
Golden dewdrops rest on the bamboo leaves outside my window.
I am recovering day by day.
Looking forward to happy days when I can work
I rest for now, a clear pool of time

○

小さい魚が
蓮の葉をつつくように
お前が来て私を吸う

○

私のさびしい生涯に
お前はみどりの翳をなげる。
窓の外にさしのべた
楓のゆれやすい枝のように
ただ形なくちらちらした光
それでいて私に無限のことを考えさす。
ほんの少しの美しい言葉や
かすかな愛のまなざしで
私のさびしい生涯を
現世に執着させる。

大いなる樹木　Ōinaru jumoku

*

Like a little fish
picking at a lotus leaf
You come to me and suckle

*

You cast a green shade
on my solitary life.
like readily swaying maple branches
stretched to my window
just a shapeless flickering light
yet you bring me thoughts of infinity.
with a few beautiful words
and a soft loving gaze
you glue my solitary life
to this world

1947. *A great big tree*

踊りの輪

美しい娘たちにまじつて
私の娘も踊っている。
人々の中にかくれて
私は彼女をみつめている。
私の結んでやった罌粟(けし)色の帯は
まだ和服に慣れない新らしい稜(かど)があって
手足のふりもひかえ気味に
彼女は連れの娘たちにまじつて踊つている。
あんまり見劣りはしないだろうか。
幸福そうにしているだろうか。
いつも手許にばかり置いて
遠くから見た事はなかったのだ。
私があれくらいの時に
抱いていた願いや夢を
彼女もやつぱり抱いているだろうか。
私のほかに誰か彼女をみているだろうか。
踊りの輪はだんだん大きくなって
唄の声は次第に高まる。
遅い月が山をはなれて
空は一めんのこまかいさざなみ雲
さざなみの皺(しわ)ごとに
銀の発光がはじまる。
やさしく進んでは歩をかえす
青もやの中の大きな花のようにぼやけて
湖水の妖精のような一群の中
もう誰が誰ともよく判らない。
美しい娘たちにまじつて
私の娘も踊っている。

美しい国　*Utsukushii kuni*

The Ring of Dancers

Along with these lovely young women
my daughter is dancing.
I am looking at her
hiding among people.
The poppy-colored sash I tied for her
shows a new fold line yet to meld with her kimono.
She is dancing along with her friends
her movements are tentative.
Is she as attractive as others?
Does she look happy?
I hadn't seen her from a distance
because I have been keeping her close to me.
I wonder if she has the wishes and dreams
which I had when I was her age.
I wonder if some people, other than myself,
are looking at her.
The ring of dancers is getting larger
the singing voices are growing louder.
The late moon left the mountain ridge
illuminating the sky with delicate rippling clouds.
Through each crease of ripples
silvery light begins to shine.
The ring moves forward a gentle step, and back a step
blurred like a large flower in pale haze.
I can no longer tell who's who
among the flock of sprites on the lake.
Along with these lovely young women
my daughter is dancing.

1948. *Beautiful country*

夜に燈(ひ)ともし

かいこがまゆをつくるように
私は私の夜をつくる。
夜を紡いで部屋をつくる。
ふかい菫色の星空のもとに
一人だけのあかりをともして
卵型の小さな世界をつくる。

昼はみんなのためにある。
私はその時何もかも忘れて働くのだ。
夜にはみんなが遠い所へ退いてしまう、
すべて見えていたものが見えなくなり
我ままな私のために
やさしく遠慮ぶかく暗い中に消えてしまう。

さびしい一人だけの世界のうちに
苔や螢のひかるように私はひかる
よい生涯を生きたいと願い
美しいものを慕う心をふかくし
ひるま汚した指で
しずかな数行を編む

苦しい熱にみちた昼の私を濾して
透明なしたたりにしてくれるもの
一たらしの夜の世界
自分のあかりをつけるさびしい小さな世界
おもいでと願いのためにある卵型の世界
一人で通る昨日とあしたのしずかな通路

美しい国　*Utsukushii kuni*

Burning a Light at Night

As a silkworm spins its cocoon
I spin my own night.
I reel off the night to build a room.
Under the deep violet-colored starry sky
I burn a light just for myself
and build a small egg-shaped world.

The daytime is there for everybody.
That's when I work forgetting everything.
At night everyone recedes to distant places.
All things visible become invisible
and to me, self-willed,
gently thoughtfully melt into the darkness.

Inside a world for myself alone
I glow as moss and fireflies do.
Wishing to live a good life
to fortify my heart's yearning for the beautiful
I knit a few quiet lines
with my fingers still soiled from my daytime work

A droplet of my nightly world,
filtering out the painful fevers of my daytime self
makes me into crystalline dewdrops
my small lonesome world lit by my own light
my egg-shaped world for recollections and wishes
a quiet pathway I take all alone between yesterday and tomorrow

1948. *Beautiful country*

美しい国

はばかることなくよい思念を
私らは語ってよいのですって。
美しいものを美しいと
私らはほめてよいのですって。
失ったものへの悲しみを
心のままに涙ながしてよいのですって。

敵とよぶものはなくなりました。
醜とよんだものも友でした。
私らは語りましょう手をとりあって
そしてよい事で心をみたしましょう

ああ長い長い凍えでした。
涙も外へは出ませんでした。
心をだんだん暖めましょう。
夕ぐれて星が一つずつみつかるように
感謝と云う言葉さえ
今やっとみつけました

私をすなおにするために
あなたのやさしいほほえみが要り
あなたのためには私のが、

ああ夜ふけて空がだんだんにぎやかになるように
瞳はしずかにかがやきあいましょう
よい想いで空をみたしましょう。
心のうちにきらめく星空をもちましょう。

美しい国　*Utsukushii kuni*

Beautiful Country

We can now speak, I hear,
good thoughts with no scruples.
We can praise, I hear,
what is beautiful as beautiful.
We can now shed tears to our heart's content
in our sorrow over what we have lost.

We no longer have enemies.
Those we called hateful turned out to be friends.
Let us talk, let us speak hand in hand
and fill our hearts with good things.

Ah, we have been under a long long freeze.
Not even tears could flow.
Let us warm our hearts steadily.
Just as we see a star and then another after the sun sets
I even found just now
the word gratitude

I need your gentle smiles
for me to be trusting
as you need mine

Ah as the sky becomes populated into the night
eyes shall softly shine to one another
Let us fill the sky with good thoughts.
Let us hold the sky filled with shining stars in our hearts.

1948. *Beautiful country*

だまして下さい言葉やさしく

だまして下さい言葉やさしく
よろこばせて下さいあたたかい声で。
世慣れぬわたしの心いれをも
受けて下さい、ほめて下さい。
ああなたには誰よりもわたしが要(い)ると
感謝のほほえみでだまして下さい。

その時わたしは
思いあがって傲慢になるでしょうか
いえいえわたしは
やわらかい蔓草のようにそれを捕えて
それを力に立ち上りましよう。
もつともつとやさしくなりましよう。
もつともつと美しく
心ききたる女子(おなご)になりましよう。

ああわたしはあまりにも荒地にそだちました。
飢えた心にせめて一つほしいものは
わたしがあなたによろこばれると
そう考えるよろこびです。
あけがたの露やそよかぜほどにも
あなたにそれが判って下されば
わたしの瞳はいきいきと若くなりましよう。
うれしさに涙をいつぱいためながら
だまされだまされてゆたかになりましよう。
目かくしの鬼を導くように
ああわたしをやさしい拍手で導いて下さい。

焔について　*Honoo ni tsuite*

Humor Me with Your Sweet Words

Humor me with your sweet words.
Please me with your warm voice.
Will you accept and compliment
my thoughtfulness for you even though I am naive?
Please humor me with your appreciative smile
to show me that you need me more than anyone else.

When you do
will I feel self-important, and become arrogant?
No, no.
I will clutch your words as if they were a tender tendril,
empowered by them, I will raise myself.
I will become more and more loving.
I will become a more and more beautiful
and thoughtful woman.

Ah I grew up in a land so barren.
The only wish I have in my deprived heart
is for the joy in believing I please you.
If you understand that even as much as
a morning dew or a breeze
my eyes will be filled with a youthful glimmer.
With joyful tears welling up in my eyes,
humored and fooled I will be enriched.
Ah, lead me with your gentle applause
as you'd lead on a blindfolded *oni** in a game of tag.

> *In a game of tag in Japan, one child is designated as "*oni*" or "It" and blindfolded by the other children, who clap their hands to tease and lead on the *oni*. A child captured by the "*oni*" becomes the next "*oni*." "*Oni*" is generally translated as ogre or demon, but in a social context it can point to a person who is intent on his/her own pursuits, which may also be artistic, worldly, or friendly, depending on circumstances.—Trans.

1950. *On flames*

女のうたえる

お友達のちっともないあなたは
私ばかりをみつめていらつしやる。
そして私をお叱りなさる。
心の足りない女だとお叱りなさる。
まだ　まだ
愛のあかしが足りない
いつも娯しそうに見えないとはけしからん
僕のために今日の天気が予言出来ないとはけしからん
私に出来ない無理ばかりお云いなさる

私は魔術を習いはじめたい。
私の一瞥であなたの批評を止めさせたい。
私は指一本であなたの心を眠らせたい。
私は箒にのつて毎夜出かけたい。
煙のように髪をなびかせながら
山の瀬を跳びこえたい。
私は彼の叱咤をわらいながら
きらめく月光の中へ飛んでゆきたい。

単純なあなたは
死ぬ程の私の苦しみを想っては下さらない。
それでいてやがて平気であなたは天国へおゆきなさる
そして魔術を念じた私は地獄へ墜ちる
ああそれで跳び越えられない百億年の距離が出来る。

焔について　　*Honoo ni tsuite*

Song of a Woman

With no friends of your own
You are looking only at me
And you accuse me.
You scold me, saying I'm not attentive enough
No, not enough
No, not enough
Not enough proof of loving you
How insolent of me not to look happy all the time
How impudent of me not to foretell today's weather for you
You always want me to do things I can't

I want to start learning witchcraft.
I want to stop your criticism with a darting look.
I want to put your heart to sleep with a flick of a finger.
I want to go out every night riding a broom.
I want to jump over the mountain ridge
Billowing my hair like smoke.
I want to fly into the sparkling moonlight
Laughing away your beratings far below.

You are so simple that
You give no thought to the pain that is almost killing me.
Yet, you will nonchalantly go to heaven by and by.
And I, having wished for witchcraft, will fall to hell
Ah, that can create ten billion years of uncrossable distance.

1950. *On flames*

木蔭の人

私はさつきから木の蔭で
あなたがじつとみていらつしやることに気づいていた
夫にいたわられて
チチアンや
ルノアールの絵のような白い輝きにみちたあなたが。

ただ一人あえぎながら
苦渋の火花の中できたえられて来た私。
今立派にすつくとつつ立つて
どうやらあなたの夫と話している私。
もう恥かしさもなく
ただ一人前の人間らしく──。
でも私は気づいている。
あなたの眸が青々と
濡れたように警戒と心配で光つているのを。
私の驕つた心がやさしくなる
女のあわれさが身にしみて
私は次第にうなだれてゆく。

ほんとにあなたの夫はすぐれた方
その前に立つことが私の小さなよろこびであることを
あなたはするどくみぬいていらつしやる。
鍛えられて私の皮膚が金色にかがやいていることを
あなたはちやんと見ていらつしやる。
その上にも私が雲のように襞多いブラウスで来たことを知ってい
　　らつしゃる。
そしてまあたらしいシャッポでいることも。
あなたは何もかもみぬこうとしていらつしやる
さびしいような潮が私の胸にこみあげる。

You in the Shade of a Tree

For some time now I have been aware
of your eyes fixed on me from the shade of a tree.
You, so fondly treasured by your husband,
are radiant with a fair glow like a Renoir
or a Titian.

I have been tempered by toilsome sparks of fires
all by myself, gasping for air.
Now I stand tall on my ground
managing to speak with your husband.
I am no longer embarrassed
I behave simply as a wholesome human being—.
Yet I am aware.
Your eyes, so blue they look dewy, glisten
with worries and apprehensions.
My proud heart grows tender
deeply moved by woman's frailty
I slowly hang down my head.

Your husband is truly exceptional;
It is a small joy for me to stand before him,
as your keen insight tells you.
You see clearly
my tempered skin glowing gold.
Beyond that, you know that I came
in a blouse with many frills like clouds.
Also you know I am wearing a brand-new hat.
You are intent on seeing through everything.
A wistful tide surges inside me.

お話出来るのがうれしいのだ。
ああ邪悪な何ものにも乱されずに──
私の心は次第々々にうなだれる。
ああどうしてだかわたしら女と云うもののあわれさに──。

焰について　*Honoo ni tsuite*

Honestly I am not trying to take anything from you.
I am simply pleased to be able to speak to him
as a self-reliant person.
Ah, not stirred by anything malicious—
My heart slowly gradually wilts.
To think, ah why is it, how frail we are, we women—.

1950. *On flames*

なぜこんなに

なぜこんなに心がいそぐのだろう
まるで十一月に枯れる一本の草のように。
まるで太陽のやさしさがなかつたら死ぬ昆虫の運命のように。
寒い風の中で私は耕す。
まるでリヤ王かマクベス風な荒天の下で。
髪をゆわえた三角巾のはしが
はたはたと耳もとで鳴る。
鳥のように叫びたいとまねて
樹々がはばたきをするように――。
私の心は唖なのだ。
手がこごえはじめる。
涙が流れはじめる。
もう誰一人見えない夕ぐれに
いつの間にかさびしく残されて、
そしてこれが私に丁度よい事と思って。

焔について　*Honoo ni tsuite*

Why Like This

Why is my heart hurried like this
as if it were a stalk of grass drying up in November
as if it were an insect fated to die without warm sunlight?
In the cold wind I till the field
under the raging sky as if in King Lear or Macbeth.
The tips of the triangular scarf tying down my hair
flutter by my ears
like a tree beating its wings
wishing to shriek like a bird—.
My mind is mute.
My hands begin to freeze.
Tears begin to fall.
In the evening not a single person is around
I am left alone before I know it
and I think this is what I deserve.

1950. *On flames*

焰について　**Flames**

焰よ
足音のないきらびやかな踊りよ
心ままなる命の噴出よ
お前は千百の舌をもつて私に語る、
暁け方のまつくらな世帯場*で――。

年毎に落葉してしまう樹のように
一日のうちにすっかり心も身体もちびてしまう私は
その時あたらしい千百の芽の燃えはじめるのを感じる。
その時私は自分の生の濁らぬ源流をみつめる。
その時いつも黄金(きん)色の詩がはばたいて私の中へ降りてくる
　　のを感じる。

焰よ
火の鬣よ
お前のきらめき、お前の歌
お前は滝のようだ
お前は珠玉のようだ。
お前は束の間の私だ。

でもその時はすぐ過ぎる
ほんの十分間。
なぜなら私は去らねばならない
まだ星のかがやいている戸の外へ水を汲みに。
そしてもう野菜をきざまねばならない。
一日を落葉のほうへいそがねばならない。
焰よ
その眼にみえぬ鉄床の上に私を打ちかがやかすものよ
わが時の間の夢殿よ。

　*世帯場＝厨

焰について　*Honoo ni tsuite*

Flames

Flames,
glorious dancers in soundless steps
eruptions of life as it pleases
you speak to me with a hundred and a thousand tongues
in the pitch dark cookery* at daybreak—.

I exhaust my heart and body within a day
like a tree that loses its leaves annually, but
at this moment I sense a hundred and a thousand new shoots being kindled.
At this moment I fix my eyes on the undisturbed source of my life.
At this moment I always sense a golden poem beating its wings descending into me.

Flames,
mane of fire,
your glow, your song
you are like waterfalls
you are like jewels
you are myself in the moment.

But that moment quickly goes by
just in ten minutes
because I must go to draw water
outdoors where stars are still shining.
And it's already time to chop vegetables.
I must hurry through the day toward the falling leaves.
Flames,
you, who beat me to make me shine on your invisible anvil,
you, the palace of my dreams for my moment.

*Cookery, where meals are prepared. In this case cooking is done on an open fire.

1950. *On flames*

渦

堪えがたく迷い又患う
それが私自身の宿運なのです
そのふかいはげしい渦が
ついあなたをいざないます
その蒼い底に私と云うものの
本当の姿がちらりとみえたと思って
あなたは私を捕えようと焦慮なさるのです
でももつと美しい私がいると思われるのは
それはあなたの錯覚です
ただ大きな渦自身が
私のかわらぬ姿ですから。
ああどうしてか私のこころに
不思議に生れる海水の段。
目も伏せ心もしずかにしていたいと思つても
すぐ何かが押しよせてくるのです
そしてとどろきやしぶきの世界になるのです
賢いけだかい女性が
導いて至高の天におつれするようには
多分私は出来ていないのです
ただ私自身の渦巻です
水平を求めるはげしい動顛です
中心にむかう盲目な速度です
私と云うものにふれようと
そんなに欲求なさいますな
もろともに生きるにはあまりにはげしい私なのです
誘うとも思わないのに
つい引きこもうとするのです
潮のなだれです　鹹い歯車です

薔薇詩集　*Bara shi shū*

Vortex

Unbearably indecisive and confused
That is my own fate
Its deep fierce vortex
Unwittingly seduces you
You think you had a glimpse of the real me
At the vortex's deep blue bottom
You get anxious trying to catch me
But it is your illusion
To think that there's a more beautiful me
I am a large vortex as always
Ah why is it that my heart mysteriously
Creates layers of ocean water
Even though I wish to be calm in my mind with my eyes closed
Something comes surging over me
And becomes a world of roar and sprays
Perhaps I am not meant to be a wise and noble woman
Who will lead you to the sublime heaven
I am simply a vortex of myself
A fierce modulation seeking equilibrium
A blind velocity seeking a center
Please do not desire me so
To touch what is me
I am too fervid for us two to survive together
I don't intend to seduce you
Yet in spite of myself I try to draw you in
I am a tidal avalanche, a caustic cogwheel

1958. *Poems of roses*

束の間

わが詩の成る　束の間
わが愛する　束の間
まつくらな世帯場で
燃える炎をみつめている束の間
ほほづえついて自分の顔も金にそめて
お釜の中には
あすのお麦が煮立っているその束の間
天から降つてくるのか
炎といつしよに私が燃えるのか
踊りゆらめくリズムの早さ
おおおお
そのくれないの光の中に
私の冠が鋳られていた。

薔薇詩集　*Bara shi shū*

The Fleeting Moment

The fleeting moment when my poetry takes shape
The fleeting moment I love
The fleeting moment when I stare into burning flames
In my pitch-dark kitchen
Propping up my chin on my hands, dyeing my face golden
That fleeting moment when barley
Is boiling in a pot for tomorrow
Does it come down from heaven?
Or am I burning along with the flames?
Quick rhythms, dancing and lilting
Oooooh
In the crimson brilliance
My crown is being forged

1958. *Poems of roses*

苗

私はかぼそい苗を植えた
私は肩にしなう肥料をかつぎ
私は汗にあえて畦泥をこね
今満々と満ち来たる山川の流れの
わが田に小さい渦をなして注ぎ入るところに
私はかぼそい苗を植えた、
我と家族の命をつながんために。
我が詩の命をもつながんために。
わが苗のそよぎの
あまりに緑うすく柔かなるがあわれさに
心にちかつて人並の百姓にならんと思うた。

薔薇詩集　*Bara shi shū*

Seedlings

I planted scrawny seedlings
I balanced bags of manure on my shoulder
I mixed and kneaded the levee mud with my sweat
I planted scrawny seedlings
Where a mountain stream, swelling now, poured
In small whirls into my rice paddy
It is to make me and my family live.
It is also to keep my poetry alive.
Pitying my seedlings
swaying, so pale and pliant
I swore to myself to become a decent farmer.

1958. *Poems of roses*

夜あけ

一日に一度ずつ色彩の無くなることは
ほんとにいいことだ、
あすのあさ鮮らしく生れ出るのを
こんなに待ちどおしくよろこぶ心を持っている私には──
この空間に在りと思われ
まだ姿をあらわさぬわがひとよ

その人が今私に見えないこともいいことだ
地球のまるみだけぼんやり見えるつめたい空気の中で
翼のない鳥のかたちの影をおとしながら
ただひとりあの樅の木が
だんだん輝いてくるのを待っているように
新しい朝の光を待ちこがれている私には──

薔薇詩集　*Bara shi shū*

Dawn

Colors disappear once each day
that is truly a good thing
for me for my heart so eagerly waiting and joyful
for their fresh birth tomorrow morning—
My love, who seems to be in this space
yet not showing yourself

It is also good that I do not see you now
in the cold air through which I just vaguely see the curve of the earth
I am so very anxiously waiting for the fresh morning light
like a lone fir tree casting its shadow shaped like a wingless bird
waiting for the new morning glow to gradually shine—

1958. *Poems of roses*

私の足に

私の足に合う靴はない。
私にぴったりする靴は
星の間にでも懸っているだろう。
私は第一靴と云うものを好かないのだ。
足の形につくって足にはめると云うことは
全く俗なことではないか。
それに奴隷的なことでさえある。
私はもつと軽くもつと翼のあるものがいい。
もつと水気があって、もつとたんわりしたものを選ぶ。
そんな風に人々はちつとも考えないのか。
ひさし髪と云うものが当然であった時もあった。
長い裾をひきずらなくては
恥かしくて歩けない時もあった
夜、星のすべすべした中に靴をさがす。
靴型星座をたずねあぐんで、
私のもすそはその時東の暁け方にふれる。
けれども夜があけて私は草の上に立っている。
私の蹠(あなうら)は大方の靴よりも美しい。
そしてこの蹠はいつも飢えているのだ。
そしていつも砂礫に血を流すのだ。

山上の死者　*Sanjō no shisha*

To Fit my Feet

No shoes fit my feet.
Shoes that would snugly fit me
may be hanging among the stars.
First of all I dislike shoes.
Isn't it just too crude to make things shaped like feet
and put your feet in them?
It's even servile.
I prefer something more airy and winged.
I would choose something more moist and pliant.
Can't people think that way at all?
There were times women were expected to wear big bulging hairdos.
There were times they would be too embarrassed to be seen
without dragging their skirts on the floor.
At night, I look for shoes in the starry smoothness.
I search for a shoe-shaped constellation in vain
then the train of my skirt touches the dawn in the East.
But once the day breaks I am standing on the grass.
My soles are more beautiful than most shoes.
And besides my soles are always hungry.
And they always bleed in gravel.

1954. *The dead on the mountaintop*

蛇

鏡の中に棲んでいる蛇よ
朝のつめたいガラスの中を泳いで
たちまちわが睫毛のかげにかくれたものよ
お前は姿みせるのをいとう
お前の含羞はすみやかに
然しお前は長く私の中に棲む。
多分かの失楽の時以来。
お前の姿は私にいつも波紋をのこす
お前は自分を毒あるかと恥じる。

なめらかにそしていたいたしいものよ
藍と朱の瞬間よ
出ておいで久しい友
美しい夏の光のいま燃える時に
わが翳より出ておあそび

ひとときの
ひとときの樹々のくるめきに
その患いをお忘れ
わが心をお前のさびしい園に。

やがて消えるこの光の中で
在ることの
何故そう苦しい？
わが姿を
人の目にもとまるまいと悩む？
或は人の心を誘うまいとおじる？

空の色
いま純粋なるきわみ
すべてのもの燃えてきよらかなるこのひとときに！

山上の死者　　*Sanjō no shisha*

Snake

Snake, you live in the mirror
you swim in the cold glass plate in the morning and
quickly hide yourself in the shade of my eyelashes
you loathe showing yourself
you are coy and swift
but you've lived inside me for a long time.
perhaps since the loss of innocence.
your presence always stirred me
you are ashamed and suspicious of your own venom.

You, slithering and pitiable one
you, a moment of indigo and vermillion
come out, my old friend,
now in the brilliant summer light aflame
come out of my shadow and play

For a moment
in a momentary vertigo of trees
leave your worries behind
leave my heart in your desolate garden.

In this light soon to be gone
why is it that
to be
is so full of pain?
are you troubled that you might be seen?
are you hesitating lest you seduce a man's heart?

The color of the sky is
now at the height of its purity
in this fresh moment after everything has gone up in flames!

1954. *The dead on the mountaintop*

私は地球

私は濁ってあたたかい土
私は一本の柔かい茎
みちべりのへびいちごの花冠にまで
私は吸いあげている私の生を——

私は一枚の泥田の水口を
もりあがって流れ入る水の乳房におどろく。
私は自分が
深い茄子紺色の大洋の底から
火と硫黄を噴きあげる熱い蒸気であることにおどろく。
私は血液の紅い流れが
人の形で地上を被うていることにおどろく。
それは海流の干満とともにあふれ
遠くみえない引力によって月々ほとばしるのにおどろく。

あわれなその形は茸（きのこ）のようにこわれやすく
一人の愛、一人の生れつきは
ペンペン草のかげで雨やどりしているようなものであるのに
私はいつか一人の男の挫折の時に
ついに押しつつむ屍衣であることにおどろく。

私ははびこり　そして地（つち）と同じだ。
沢山の挫折と沢山の空費は
土の中の小さい蛆たちや人知れぬ崖ぶちにゆれる水仙たちと同
　　じだ。

I Am the Earth

I am warm, turbid earth
I am a single supple stalk
I pump my life
all the way up into corollas of wild berries on the roadside—

I am amazed at
a breast of water welling to flow into the inlet of a muddy rice paddy.
I am amazed at
myself being
hot steam blowing up fire and sulfur
from the bottom of the great ocean, deep indigo.
I am amazed at
the crimson blood flow
covering the earth's surface in human shape.
I am amazed that it swells as the tides ebb and flow, and
gushes out monthly under distant invisible gravity.

Its pitiable shape is as fragile as a mushroom
one's love, one's being, is
as helpless as seeking shelter from the rain under a shepherd's purse,
yet I am amazed at myself having become the shroud that finally
    envelops a man
at the time of his defeat.

I luxuriate and I am earth itself.
I share countless setbacks and immense waste
with tiny maggots in the dirt and
with daffodils quivering at the edges of unknown cliffs.

私は私が脈ある夕ぐれであることにおどろく。
私は私が稲の葉先に時をきめて昇る水玉であることにおどろく。

私は地球だ。
そこに生きていてそしてそのものと同じだ。

四十億年目に
私のネガ　私の異性
永遠のつめたい月に気づいた時
私ははじめて自分があたたかい泥であることにおどろく。

海は陸へと　*Umi wa riku e to*

I am amazed that I am the pulsating twilight.
I am amazed that I am a dewdrop which rises at a set time to the
    blade tip of a rice plant.

I am the Earth.
I live there, and I am the very same Earth.

In the four billionth year
when I have come to know my other self, my alter ego,
the eternal cold moon,
I am amazed, for the first time, that I am warm mud.

1972. *The sea toward the land*

第三の眼

あけがたに
生れたばかりの嬰児をかたえに
やさしいサフラン色の娘は横たわっている。
その娘を生んだ私の日が
まだ昨日のように絵の中にあると思うのに
その額ぶちはいつのまにか空虚になっていた。
母子像の波うつ髪は
いま娘の上にある。
額の外から皺の多い手をさしのべている老いた天使は私だ。

いつの間にか来ている
老と云うのは何だろうか。
老とは時間にめざめる事ではないのだろうか。
眉のようにやわらかい若葉の中にも
朽ちてあらわな葉脈の条理が
ルインのように透いてみえること――
それが私らの得たものではないだろうか。

この夏の光の輪が
まだ幹におどっているまに
私はかどかどの霜の小径につまづくのだ。
豊穣な酒のしたたる
葡萄棚のとり入れにさしのばすのは
凍るような月夜の骨です。

A Third Eye

At dawn
Next to her newborn
Lies my gentle daughter in saffron color.
Even though I feel my day of her birth
Is still in the picture just like yesterday
Its frame has been emptied while I was unaware.
The wavy hair in the picture of a mother and child
Now belongs to my daughter.
An aged angel holding out her wrinkled hand from outside the frame
　—that's me.

What is this old age
Sneaking up on us?
Isn't aging coming to know Time?
To see decayed and bared veins like ruins
Even in a tender young leaf-shaped eyebrow—
Isn't that a gift to us from aging?

While this ring of summer's light
Is dancing on the tree trunk
I trip over a frosty angular trail.
To harvest grapes off the vines
Dripping with rich wine, I stretch out
My bones in the freezing moonlit night.

老とはきつと
心をゆりさますふしぎな第三の眼が
額の上にきざまれることだ。
そこから射す光線は
帽子のダイヤをまわすように
物体のかげに時間のせせらぎをみせるのだ。

生れた嬰児の半透明の小さな指のかたちに
ひなげしの種子のようにきっちりと
小さな爪がならんでいる。
それはなぜ電気のように私をふるわすのか。
いとしさと耐えがたさは重なるのか。
流れた時の量や距離の反射に
思わず第三の眼がまばたくのだ。

時は深い井戸のようにちらめいて
母子像は水底にみえる。

月は白髪のままにのぼって来て
「そうだろう、朋(とも)よ」としずかに云う。
そしてその光は私の肩をいだく。
第三の眼をもつものは
つねにふしぎな望遠鏡をのぞいて
おののいているさびしい天使の仲間なのだ。

海は陸へと　*Umi wa riku e to*

Aging perhaps means
Sculpting on one's forehead
A mysterious third eye that shakes and wakes the heart.
The rays of light shooting from the eye
As if from a diamond on a turning hat
Illuminate Time rippling, in the shadows of things.

The tiny nails are lined up
Neatly arranged like field-poppy seeds
Tracing the small opaque fingers of the newborn.
Why do they make me tremble like electricity?
Do love and unbearable feelings converge?
My third eye blinks in spite of me
At the reflection of the volume and distance of Time that has passed.

Time flickers like a deep well
Showing the image of a mother and child at its bottom.

The moon rises in its gray hair
And calmly says, "Isn't that so, my friend?"
And its light hugs my shoulders.
One with a third eye
Is the friend of a lonely angel quivering
Always peering into a mysterious telescope.

1972. *The sea toward the land*

石炭と思って

石炭と思って燃していたものは命であった。
靴と思ってふんだものは血のつづく蹠(あなうら)であつた。
指を切って畝に蒔き
心臓をきざんで家畜に与えた。

風が樹々の竜骨を喬く揚げる時
彼等と共に夜じゆう巨浪をのりこえた。
あすの朝こそ私は薔薇の蕾になろう
あすの朝こそつめたく散る滝になろう
その祈りで年を経た。

雲間に心を射るような瞳がみえた
と思ったら
それは新月の昇つてくるのだった。
目にもとまらぬ速さであじさい色の空を泳ぎのぼる
おおあの月が西の天末に
しずかにしたたり落ちるまでに
私は自分と見わけもつかぬ泥の上衣をぬいで
しばし茨の床に自分をやすませよう。

海は陸へと　*Umi wa riku e to*

Believing It Was Coal

It was my life that I was burning, believing it was coal
It was the fleshy sole of my foot that I stepped on thinking it was a shoe
I cut off my fingers and planted them in the furrows
I chopped up my heart and fed it to farm animals

When the wind lifted up the keels of the trees
I rode gigantic waves with them through the night.
Tomorrow morning at last, may I be a rosebud
Tomorrow morning at last, may I be the cool cascade of a waterfall
Thus I prayed as time passed

Among clouds, I thought I saw
An eye shooting at my heart
But it was the new moon rising.
It is swimming up the hydrangea-colored sky at blinding speed
Oh until the moon silently drips down
To the western end of heaven
I shall shed my robe of mud indistinguishable from myself and
Rest myself on a thorny bed for a time.

1972. *The sea toward the land*

ライバルは「死」であった
　　──竜巻のらめんと

おもかげはいま波だっていて
私の水面は静まらない
あなたはどこにでもいたから
逢わなくても心は安らかだった
遠い凝視は私の足どりを軽くし
茨の中さへ静かに歩けた

だのにもうその人はいない
彼が「死」に捕われ去ったときいた時
竜巻のように私の心は空へ縒(よ)れあがる
おお私を被っていた手はいま去った
その見えない空洞の芯をめぐって
紐のようによじれて高く巻き揚がる宙の道よ
高く　けれど羽によってでなく
ただ砂につづく熱い執着としてのみそれは移る──

今日私が歩んでいるのはそのように重く
いずこを指してか、人目にはただしなやかにゆるやかに ──
捕われは空間に瞬間の光る痕のみを残し
ライバルは「死」であった
彼が去ってまだ半月にすぎないことを茫然といぶかしむ
すでに焦悴は私の形を変えた
雲が一つの形を保ち得ないで雨降るように
私はすべての部分から溶解し雨降る
その微妙な　そして広漠とした全体よ
無限と釣合っているわが牽引よ
レエテにまで降りそそぐわが悲しみは
ささえかねて
低く地にただよい
鉛色なる霧に紛(ま)ごう

続永瀬清子詩集　*Zoku Nagase Kiyoko shi shū*

My Rival Was Death
   —The lament of the whirlwind

Your image is now rippling
My mind's fluid surface will not be calmed
Because you were everywhere
My mind was at peace even though we did not meet
Your intense gaze from the distance used to lighten my gait and
I could walk calmly even through thorns

Yet, the man is no more
When I heard Death captured and took him away
My heart spun up into the sky like a whirlwind
Oh his hands that have enveloped me are gone now
Oh a cosmic path whirling up high in mid-air, twisting like a ribbon
Circling around the core of this invisible hollow
It soars high, moving not on wings but only
As a fevered devotion tied to sand—

Today I walk with such a heavy gait
But to where? Others may see me simply supple and slow—
My obsession left only a momentary shining scar in mid-air, and
My rival was Death
Absently I marvel it's a mere half-month since he's gone
Debility has already changed what I am
Just as a cloud cannot hold its shape to let it rain
I dissolve from all corners and turn into rain
The delicate and all encompassing totality
My attraction equals the infinite!
My sorrows, pouring even over Lethe,
Unable to bear up
Waft low on the ground
Fuse into lead-colored fog

1982. *Poems of Nagase Kiyoko II*

あけがたにくる人よ

あけがたにくる人よ
ててっぽっぽうの声のする方から
私の所へしずかにしずかにくる人よ
一生の山坂は蒼くたとえようもなくきびしく
私はいま老いてしまって
ほかの年よりと同じに
若かった日のことを千万遍恋うている

その時私は家出しようとして
小さなバスケット一つをさげて
足は宙にふるえていた
どこへいくとも自分でわからず
恋している自分の心だけがたよりで
若さ、それは苦しさだった

その時あなたが来てくれればよかったのに
その時あなたは来てくれなかった
どんなに待っているか
道べりの柳の木に云えばよかったのか
吹く風の小さな渦に頼めばよかったのか

To You Who Come at Dawn

You who come at dawn,
You come to where I am, quietly, quietly
from where doves call
nothing compares with my life's ups and downs, steep and blue
I have grown old
millions of times I have yearned for the days of my youth,
just as other old people do

at that time I was about to run away from home
carrying a single wicker basket
I was shaking, feet not touching the ground
I had no idea where to go
relying only on
my heart in love
youthfulness was a torment

I wish You had come at that time
but You did not come at that time
should I have told a willow by the roadside
how anxiously I was waiting for You to come?
should I have begged a little dust devil for help?

あなたの耳はあまりに遠く
茜色の向うで汽車が汽笛をあげるように
通りすぎていってしまった

もう過ぎてしまった
いま来てもつぐなえぬ
一生は過ぎてしまったのに
あけがたにくる人よ
ててっぽっぽうの声のする方から

私の方へしずかにしずかにくる人よ
足音もなくて何しにくる人よ
涙流させにだけくる人よ

あけがたにくる人よ　*Akegata ni kuru hito yo*

Your ears, so far away,
passed by
like a train blowing its whistle beyond the evening glow

all is in the past now
it won't do any good if You come now
my life has passed, yet
You come at dawn

softly, gently
toward me from where doves call
for what? Your footsteps make no sound
You come merely to make my tears flow

1987. *To you who come at dawn*

老いたるわが鬼女

私の洞(ほこら)に棲む老いたる鬼女は
冷い霜の朝に咳(しわぶき)ながら
朝日と苔のあいだにみえかくれする

わがグレンデルの母親よ
哭きながら王の城をおびやかし
その驕れる宴を蹴ちらし
その棟に高くかかげられていた
わが子の腕をとり返した――
又、手むかう武士たちの首を
藁束のように摑んであざ笑った――
野をひとり奔りゆくもの
雨雲のように髪をなびかすもの
百合はたおれ
あざみは血に濡れ――

あけがたの光の中に
ひとり自由、孤り輝く高貴(サブライム)
彼女の胸に一人の王者なく
彼女のほかに一片の掟もない
野の獣を食いその毛皮をまとい
心は暗く裂かれ　身をきざんでいたが
歯は北海に寄せる　波のように白く高笑った

My Aged Demon

The aged demon dwells in my cavern
Clears her throat on cold frosty mornings
Goes in and out of sight between the morning sun and the moss

You, my dear Grendel's mother,
You terrorized the King's castle as you loudly wept
You broke up his arrogant feast
And took back your son's arm
Hung high from the beam—
You grabbed the necks of resisting warriors
As if they were bundles of straw and you sneered at them—
You dashed through the wilderness alone
Streaming your hair like rain clouds
Lilies fell
Thistles were drenched in blood—

In the light at dawn
She was sublime, shining alone, free on her own
Not a single King on her mind
Not a single rule except herself
She ate wild beasts and wore their furs
Her heart was torn darkly, and her flesh was tormented
Yet she roared loud in laughter
Showing her teeth as white as the waves beating on the north shore

いつの日からか　私の洞に棲んでいる老いたる鬼女
おお　それは彼女か
みやびなく華やかさなく、
磨(と)いでいるのはただ我執の牙、
銅色の髪はすでに枯色
眼(まなこ)のみ赤らみ皺に埋れんとして
なおまだ思っている若き日日の自由、
わが足はあの丘の上の樺の木のように立っているが
いまは跳躍して谷を越す由もない

満天の星の下、わが洞になおいささかの霜をさけて
昔のよき日の夢をあたためる

目ざむれば　しわぶきしつつ
わが老いたる鬼女は
薄き粥煮んと
苔のかなたに見えかくれする

あけがたにくる人よ　*Akegata ni kuru hito yo*

The aged demon has lived in my cavern, since when I don't know
Oh, is that her
Whetting the blade of egoism
With no grace, no brilliance
Her copper-colored hair has dried up
Only her eyes are red nearly hidden by wrinkles
Still longing for the freedom of her youth

My legs are planted like birch trees on the hill
And there's no jumping across the valley

Under the sky full of stars, hiding in my cavern to avoid a little frost
She warms dreams of her good old days

As she wakes up, clearing her throat
My aged demon
Goes in and out of sight beyond the moss
Ready to cook watery gruel

1987. *To you who come at dawn*

黙っている人よ　藍色の靄よ

もう土の中に入ってしまった人よ
ひがな一日黙っていまは
しめっぽい所にじっとしている人よ

詩を書く私はいつも自分一人になり切ろうとして
ほかのことは何も考えられなかったから
あなたはきっと　とても淋しかったわ

あなたは私を乱すまいと離れて私をみていた
それがあなたの藍色の愛だったのに
私はそれをまるで思いもしなかった

　　　私は今はもう本当のひとりになったのだから
　　　私はいつでも自由にはばたけるのに
　　　なぜかふしぎにあなたがすぐそばにいるみたい

あなたここにほんとにいて下さいと
云えばひとりでに涙が流れるわ
生きている時　云えもしなかったその言葉

　　　悪い妻　心なしの私は
　　　できるだけあなたに尽したいとは思っても
　　　つい遠い夢の方へ心がいったわ

My Dear Silent One, My Indigo Mist

My dear, you've gone into the earth
you are silent now all day long
motionless in a damp place

I, a poet, always tried to be by myself
and could not think of anything else
so you must have been very lonely

not wanting to distract me you were watching me from a distance
that was your love in indigo color
but I never even thought about it

>since I am truly by myself now
>I can freely beat my wings at any time
>yet, oddly, I feel you right next to me

please be with me here for real—
saying that makes my tears flow of their own accord
I couldn't bring myself to say those words while you were alive

>a bad wife, heartless me
>even though I wanted to do my best to be good to you
>my heart somehow drifted to distant dreams

でも世の中の男の人は
どんなに大きな岩みたいな仕事を彫りあげても
そのため妻に不在を詫びようとは思わないのに

　　私はただ柔かな身近な泥をこねていただけなのに
　　なぜこうも可愛想でたまらないの
　　あなたの方ばかりに私が向いていなかったことが——

つまらない女　くず女
あなたは土の中で
たとえ　いいんだよと云ったとしても

　　枕元によみさしの本をがらくたのように積んで
　　夜中に眼ざめてその一冊をとりあげる
　　それが時々地くずれするわ蝶がとびたつふうに

私を生かそうと願っていたわ
すこし離れていまも見ているのね
いいえ死んだのだからもっと近くにいるよと云いたいのね

　　世の中に適しないで誰の群にも交わらず
　　あなたは山椒魚のようにたった一人いたのね
　　岩かげでただ私だけをみつめていた人よ　藍色の靄よ

だましてください言葉やさしく　*Damashite kudasai kotoba yasashiku*

but a man in this world
doesn't even dream of apologizing to his wife for his absence
for his work, however gigantic a rock he may have carved

    I was simply kneading some malleable and familiar mud
    why do I feel so sorry
    that my heart was not singly attentive to you—?

I am a worthless woman, a good-for-nothing woman
even if you say "That's ok" to me
from inside the earth

    I have half-read books piled like a junk-heap by my bed
    I awake in the middle of the night and pick one up
    at times the pile flies to the floor like butterflies trying to take off

your wish was to let me live
even now, keeping a little distance, you are watching me, aren't you?
rather, you want to say, you are closer to me because you are dead,
    right?

    misfit in this world, belonging to no group
    you were all by yourself like a salamander
    you were looking only at me from the shadow of rocks, my dear,
    my indigo mist

2008. *Humor me with your sweet words*

短章

トラックが来て私を轢いた時

　トラックが来て私を轢いた時、私の口からは「飢えたる魂」がとび出す。私の肋骨からははめられていた格子が解かれて「自由」が流れだす。
　トラックが轢かないうちは、それはただの他人とみわけがつかない。
　だから詩を書くことはトラックに轢かれる位の重さだと知ってもらいたい。あんまり手軽には考えてほしうない。

詩人とは何か

　詩人とは何か。
　詩人とは誰よりも正直な人でなければならない。
　人間の精神について、自分の存在について、誰よりも正直に語る
　　ために嘘をまなぶ。

詩を書く理由

植物の中を水が通るように──。
つまり植物の表面において水は乾くから、
植物は根から水を汲むポンプだから
だから私の中を詩が通る。
かわく作用がなければ水は揚がらない。
汲む力がなければ水は通らない。
そしてそれは私の心の小さな手押ハンドルなのだ。
地球の水を汲む私の手押ハンドルなのだ。

Aphorisms

When a Truck Comes and Runs Over Me

When a truck comes and runs over me, "hungry soul" pops out of my mouth. From my ribs as the jail fence breaks "Freedom" flows out.
Before the truck runs over me, no one can tell me apart from ordinary people.
So I want you to know that writing poetry is as weighty as having a truck run over me. I don't want you to take it lightly.

What Is a Poet?

What is a poet?
A poet must be more honest than anyone else.
In order to speak more honestly than anyone else
    about the soul of mankind, about one's own being
    a poet masters lying

Why I Write Poetry

Just as water courses through a plant—.
Because water dries on a plant's surface, and
Because a plant is a pump drawing water up through its roots
So does poetry course through me.
If there's no drying action, the water will not move up.
If there's no force to pump the water, the water will not circulate.
I have a small pump handle in my mind.
My pump handle lets me draw water from the Earth.

詩は

　葉緑素が、太陽を捕えるのと同じものだ。

詩にリズムが

　詩にリズムが必要であることは、おどるためではなくて精神の壁にきざみつける方法だからだ。リズムは錐だ。

短章集　*Tanshō shu*

Poetry Is

It is identical to chlorophyll capturing the Sun.

Poetry Needs Rhythm

Poetry needs rhythm, not for dancing, but
as a tool to carve into the wall of the heart. Rhythm is an ice pick.

2007. Aphorisms

A NOTE ON TRANSLATION

I have been asked how I approached the challenge of translating poets with diverse themes, voices, and styles so that their differences come across in English. This question led me to consider what I believe poetry in translation can or should be, and to analyze how I work to achieve my goals.

My translation process is simple: concentrate on the poem at hand. Once I pick a poem to translate, I read it multiple times, trying to get in sync with the poet's genius. It is a twofold journey into the depth of the poem. In the first place it involves a search through a verbal web for what may be hiding among the words and between the lines, looking at how the poet is working or playing with the language and its power of suggestion, inference, or reference. At the same time I must delve into the creator's psyche, following the voice of the poem to see where it takes me. Each poem has its own voice. The voice may be that of the poet, a narrator, a character, an omniscient presence, or any combination of them. My task is to bring that voice into English.

When I feel ready to verbalize my experience of the poem from reading it in Japanese, I start writing in English as I reread the original lines. I try to stay mindful of the flow of the Japanese text, while conveying in English my sense of the poet's creative mind at work. This step is charged with bilingual and bicultural tension, as I am attempting to reproduce in English the intent of the Japanese words and sentences. The result is a first draft of the translation. This draft goes through multiple revisions and rewrites, to bring it closer to the original's substance and power.

When a number of translations of individual poems by one poet are pulled together, as a group they should present a multidimensional view of the author's unique creative world, including his or her temperament, concerns, and stylistic preferences at the time of writing. This assumes that the spirit and expression of the translations are as close to the original as possible. Above all, however, I have faith in the power and energy of great poetry to assert itself and lead me to produce a rendition clearly indicative of the distinctive force and depth of the original.

Thinking back, I grew up reading Japanese translations of poetry and novels from many foreign countries. When I was enjoying Goethe and Schiller, Poe, or Byron in Japanese, I read them as poetry, oblivious of their being translations, accepting the Japanese words as those of the poet. Those words spoke to me and stimulated my imagination, creating a world of their own.

But now I am aware of the translator's predicament, which is so precisely expressed by the great poet and translator W.S. Merwin:

> [I]f we take a single word of any language and try to find an exact equivalent in another, even if the second language is closely akin to the first, we have to admit that it cannot be done. A single primary denotation may be shared; but the constellation of secondary meanings, the moving rings of associations, the etymological echoes, the sound and its own levels of association, do not have an equivalent because they cannot. If we put two words of a language together and repeat the attempt, the failure is still more obvious. Yet if we continue, we reach a point where some sequence of the first language conveys a dynamic unit, a rudiment of form. Some energy of the first language begins to be manifest, not only in single words but in the charge of their relationship. The surprising thing is that at this point the hope of translation does not fade altogether, but begins to emerge.[1]

As a practitioner of translation, Merwin knows that it is impossible to transport poetry in its linguistic entirety into another language. But

---

1. W.S. Merwin, *W.S. Merwin Selected Translations 1948–2011* (Port Townsend, Washington: Copper Canyon Press, 2013) 168.

referencing the then-trendy practice among some American poets in the late 1950s and early 1960s of taking liberties with the originals to "remake" foreign poetry in English, Merwin asserts his intent to pursue fidelity in translation: "But I came to the conclusion that the word *translation* should be more responsibly used, to represent as clearly as possible some aspects of the original. I went on translating poems ... conveying whatever I was able to evoke of the sense of life of the original words."[2]

I have had the great good fortune to work with W.S. Merwin on some collaborative translation projects. While working with him I was struck by how respectful and humble he is toward the original work and its author. I try to practice Merwin's principled approach in my translation work. I believe that it is my duty to capture and deliver what the original text presents and connotes as faithfully and completely as possible in order to "evoke ... the sense of life of the original words."

This goes beyond simply focusing on words and sentences in poetry. I firmly believe that poetry can be transmitted across languages through translations that preserve its core. The core of poetry, at its deepest level, is rooted in fundamentals of humanity, such as love and hate, joy and sorrow, fear, anger, or relief. These are the common experiences of all peoples, regardless of culture, language, or temporal confines. Circling around this core in each poem is a world of the original poet's imagination, which has life and energy of its own. Trying to capture it in a translation is a challenge I enjoy.

---

2. Ibid., 292.

CHRONOLOGY OF POETS' LIVES

MURŌ SAISEI

1889   Born in Kanazawa on the Japan Sea coast to former retainer of a feudal lord and housemaid. Adopted by local priest and his verbally abusive common-law wife.

1895   Enters elementary school.

1902   Quits seventh grade, starts working as an errand boy at Kanazawa District Court. Works there in various capacities for eight years.

1903   Begins to write haiku with guidance from workplace supervisor Kawakami Fūkotsu. Devotes himself to reading, hopes to become a writer. Welcomed and appreciated as a talented youth at local haiku gathering.

1907   Attends haiku gatherings, submits haiku to open forum in local newspaper and submits poems to *Shinsei* (New Voices). Aspires to become poet.

1909   Moves to work in a registry office in a coastal town, allowing him to leave adoptive mother's house. Devotes himself to poetry, writing many poems later included in *Jojō shōkyoku shū* (Lyrical songs).

1910   Goes to Tokyo to become a poet, but lack of money forces him to return to Kanazawa. Travels back and forth between Tokyo and hometown for several years depending on financial situation. *Subaru* (Pleiades) literary magazine publishes his poems.

1913–1915   *ZAMBOA* magazine publishes his poems in every issue from January through May 1913. Impressed by Murō's poems in the magazine, Hagiwara Sakutarō starts life-long friendship with him based on shared passion for lyrical poetry. Poems were published in many literary magazines such as *Sōsaku* (Creative work), *Shiika* (Poetry), *Araragi* (Yew tree).

1916 Founds Kanjō shisha (Sentiments Poetry Press) with Hagiwara Sakutarō in 1916, which publishes magazine *Kanjō* (Sentiments). Its July and August issues, titled "Lyrical Songs," are dedicated to Murō's poetry, comprised of sixty of his lyrical poems written since his early days in Kanazawa.

1918 Self-publishes first book of poems, *Ai no shi shū* (Poems of love) through Sentiments Poetry Press. Marries Tomiko, an elementary school teacher who also writes poetry and *tanka*. Self-publishes *Jojō shōkyoku shū* (Lyrical songs).

1919–1920 Publishes *Zoku ai no shi shū* (Poems of love II) through Bunbudō Publishing. Announces he "has nothing left for poetry." Reads fiction voraciously, soon starts publishing his own novels in rapid succession, becoming a famed novelist.

1921 Son, Hyōtarō, is born in May.

1922 Hyōtarō dies in June, a severe blow to Murō. Publishes *Bōshun shi shū* (Poems of lost spring) in December, through Kyōbunsha. Turns to children's literature and essays, and devotes himself to gardening and antiques.

1923 Book of poetry *Aoki uo o tsuru hito* (A man fishing blue fish) published by Ars Press. First daughter, Asako, is born. Moves back to Kanazawa with family after Great Kantō Earthquake. Now successful and well-to-do, supports his openly grateful adoptive mother.

1924 *Kōrai no hana* (Korean flowers), a book of poems, is published by Shinchōsha.

1926   Supports literary magazine *Roba* (Donkey), launched by lyrical poets and admirers such as Hori Tatsuo and Nakano Shigeharu to provide a venue for lyrical poets as well as leftist writers.

1928   Receives Literary Award from Japan Writers Association. Book of poems *Tsuru* (Cranes) is published by Sojinsha. Hagiwara Sakutarō brings Miyoshi Tatsuji to meet him.

1930   Book of poems, *Tori suzume shū* (Birds and sparrows), is published by Daiichishobō.

1932   *Kurogane shū* (Iron poems) is published by Shiinokisha.

1933   *Jūku haru shi shū* (Poems from the spring of nineteen) is published by Shiinokisha.

1936   Publishes book of poetry *Jū hen ka* (Ten returning flowers) through Shin'yōsha. Fourteen-volume *Murō Saisei zenshū* (Collected works of Murō Saisei) is published by Hibonkaku.

1937   Tours Manchuria and Ha'erbin area of China for a month; is captivated by vast, barren continental landscape.

1940–1945   Starts to write numerous novels with ancient aristocratic motifs and many stories for young adults and children. Maintains that writers should produce new works even under hardships of war. Moves with his family to Karuizawa in 1944 as air raids intensify; does not move back to Tokyo until 1949.

1947   Publishes a book of poems, *Tabibito* (Travelers), through Usuishobō; *Murō Saisei jisen shishū* (Muro Saisei: poet's own selection) through Takagirishoin; book of poems *Ainureba* (Encounters) through Fugakuhonsha.

1948   Named a member of Japan Academy of Arts. Publishes four novels.

1951   Publishes *Murō Saisei shi shō* (Murō Saisei: selected poems) through Kantōsha and *Murō Saisei shishū* (Poems of Murō Saisei) in a Shinchō Pocket Edition.

1953   *Gendai nihon meishi sen, Jōjō shōkyoku shū / Ai no shi shū* (Lyrical songs and poems of love: great works of modern Japanese poetry) published by Chikumashobō.

1954   Hospitalized with gastric ailment for a month. *Murō Saisei shishū* (Poems of Murō Saisei) published in Atene Pocket Edition.

1955   *Murō Saisei shishū* (Poems of Murō Saisei) in Iwanami Pocket Edition.

1957   *Harubin shi shū* (Ha'erbin poems) through Tōjishobō.

1959   Citation and Gift to celebrate his seventieth birthday from Japan Writers' Association in April. Award and gift to recognize his lifetime contribution to modern poetry from Modern Poets Association in May. Publishes *Kinō irasshitte kudasai* (Please come back yesterday) from Satsukishobō. Wife Tomiko dies at sixty-four. Establishes "Murō Saisei Award for Poets."

1961   Monument to his poetic achievement is completed; later serves as his tombstone. Illness takes him in and out of hospitals.

1962   Finishes revising and editing *Murō Saisei zenshishū* (Complete poems of Murō Saisei), published by Chikumashobō. Dies in a hospital in Tokyo in March.

1964   Twelve-volume *Murō Saisei zenshū* (Complete works of Murō Saisei) published by Shinchōsha.

KANEKO MITSUHARU

1895   Born in Aichi prefecture to bankrupt brewery-heir family.

1897   Adopted by Kaneko Sōtarō, a thirty-year-old company executive and his sixteen-year-old wife who treats him like a doll. Grows up as overly sensitive child who loves to paint.

1898   Moves with family to Kyoto. Kyoto's beauty of nature and weight of tradition make strong impression on him.

1901   Enters public elementary school.

1905   Family moves to Tokyo. Baptized at a local Christian church. Takes lessons in Japanese-style painting from well-known *ukiyo-e* artist, raising expectations of his becoming a great painter.

1906   Transfers to another local public school, loses all interest in study, schemes with friend to run away to America, but they only reach nearby port, and are brought home

1907   Enters middle school. His academic ranking is high, and he competes for school's top ranking in painting.

1909   Begins skipping classes to visit library and read Chinese classics. Voracious reading extends to historical and popular novels of premodern era—collects several thousand volumes of Edo period literature in original publications along with Chinese literature. Cuts nearly two hundred school days and has to repeat grade.

1912   Along with classmates, creates and circulates mimeographed coterie magazine for which he attempts a few short stories. Devoted reader of decadent novels of the time; frequents pleasure houses posing as a novelist.

1913   Enters Waseda University English literature department. Identifies with Oscar Wilde's *Dorian Gray* and Mikhail Artsybashev's *Sanin* to the point of trying to live like those decadent characters.

1915   Leaves Waseda, dissatisfied with literature department's strong bias toward naturalism. Enters Japanese-style painting department of Tokyo Fine Arts College but hardly attends classes. Enters English literature department of Keiō University. Examining doctor at his draft physical tells him he won't last another year. Develops pneumonia, forced to stay in bed for three months.

1916   At friend's suggestion, begins to write poetry while ill in bed, finishing about thirty pieces. Reads works by emerging poets Murō Saisei and Hagiwara Sakutarō along with translations of European poetry. Publishes two issues of coterie magazine *Kōzu* (Composition). Leaves Keiō University.

1917   Adoptive father dies, leaving sizeable estate. Splits inheritance with adoptive mother but fritters away his fortune in a few years.

1918   Reading Walt Whitman's poetry and Carpenter's "Toward Democracy" opens his eyes to humanity, democracy, and democratic ideals, causing him to shed decadence.

1919   Self-publishes *Akatsuchi no ie* (House of red clay) but receives little notice from poets or readers. Leaves for first European tour at invitation of an antique dealer friend of his late adoptive father.

1920   Stays in London for a few months, moves to rural village near Brussels, enjoys reading, writing poetry, taking walks, associating with local people. Studies Belgian and French poets, including Emile Verhaeren, Albert-Victor Samain, Henri de Regnier, Baudelaire, Alfred de Musset, taking in contemporary European romanticism, symbolism, mysticism. Moves to Paris.

1921   Sails for home with ten notebooks of draft poems. Deeply impressed by encounters with Asian and South Asian scenery and people on his return voyage. Intoxicated by European culture and literature, he has hard time reacclimating to life in Japan. Concentrates on editing, revising his poems.

1923   Publishes *Koganemushi* (Gold beetle), a collection of poems written in Europe, through Shinchōsha. The book is highly praised as "a marriage of the East and the West."

1924   Marries Mori Michiyo, an aspiring novelist, with Murō Saisei as *nakōdo* (witness or go-between).

1925   Publishes book of translations, *Veruha-ran shishū* (Poems by Emile Verhaeren), from Shinchō sha. First son is born, and poverty-stricken, he and his wife move in with Michiyo's family for five months, including a month-long trip to Shanghai. Book of translations, *Kindai furansu shishū* (Early modern French poetry), is published by Kōgyokudō.

1926   Book of poems *Mizu no rurō* (Vagrant water) is published by Shinchōsha, but does not attract attention in the shadow of emerging anarchist and leftist poetry.

1928   Leaves literary aspirations behind and sets out on overseas trip with wife Michiyo. Initially intended to be short respite, the trip extends to five years.

1929   Holds exhibits of his paintings in Singapore to earn money for survival. Travels with Michiyo to Java and Malaya.

1930   Settling in Paris, couple struggles to survive for two years, taking any conceivable job for food, with no time to read books.

1932   Returns to Japan by way of Singapore and Malaya. Starts writing poems. As oppression intensifies under military control, he dodges censorship to publish subversive poems.

1935   His poem "*Same*" (Sharks) is printed in magazine *Bungei* (Literary art) on Nakano Shigeharu's recommendation. Publishes antiwar poems in a progressive general magazine *Chūō Kōron*, known for discovering new writers.

1937   Publishes *Same* (Sharks), book of heavily camouflaged antiwar protest poems from Jin'min sha.

1938   Spends one month in China touring battlefields.

1943   Moves with family to cottage in Yamanashi in the foothills of Mount Fuji to avoid air raids.

1946   Moves back to Tokyo. Begins active writing career.

1948   Publishes *Rakkasan* (Parachutes) through Nihon miraiha hakkōsho and *Ga* (Moths) through Hokutoshoin.

1949   *On'na tachi e no eregii* (Elegy for women) published by Sōgensha; another book of poems, *Oni no ko no uta* (Songs of the ogre's children) is published by Jūjiyashoten.

1952   Kaneko's translation of *Les fleurs du mal* by Baudelaire is published by Hōbunkan. His book of original poems *Ningen no higeki* (Tragedy of man) is published by Sōgensha, and receives the fifth Yomiuri Literary Award.

1955   Book of poems *Hijō* (Heartless) is published by Shinchōsha.

1956   Book of poems *Suisei* (Fluid energy) is published by Sōgensha.

1957   Autobiography *Shijin* (Poet) is published by Heibonsha.

1960   Four-volume *Kaneko Mitsuharu zenshū* (Complete works of Kaneko Mitsuharu) is published by Eureka (vol.1) and Shōrinsha (vols. 2–4).

1962   Book of poems *He no yōna uta* (Poems like farts) is published by Shichōsha.

1965   Book of poems *IL* is published from Keisōshobō.

1966   Receives Rekitei Award for *IL*. Publishes part of unpublished book of poems *Doro no hon* (Book of mud) in poetry magazines *Ainame* (Rock trout) and *Gendai no me* (Current view), expressing fierce opposition to Vietnam War.

1967   Book of poems *Wakaba no uta* (Poems of young leaves) from Keisoshobō. *Teihon Kaneko Mitsuharu zenshishū* (Authorized complete poems of Kanako Mitsuharu) is published by Chikumashobō.

1968   Book of poems *Aijō 69* (Love 69) through Chikumashobō.

1969   Book of Poems *Yogoreteinai ichinichi* (One pristine day) is published by Ainamekai.

1973   Book of Poems *Hana to akibin* (Flowers and empty bottles) is published by Seigashobō.

1975   Writes his will in April. Dies from acute heart failure in June. *Kaneko Mitsuharu zenshū* (Complete works of Kaneko Mitsuharu, 15 volumes) is published by Chūōkōronsha (1975–1977).

MIYOSHI TATSUJI

1900   Born oldest son of ten children to a family with small printing business in Osaka.

1906   Given up for adoption, which falls through due to regulations on adoption of first born sons. Taken in by his grandparents, lives with them for five years.

1907   Enters local elementary school.

1908   Suffers first nervous breakdown (from fear of death and isolation), takes long leave from school.

1911   Returns to his own family and transfers to a new school.

1913   Suffers another nervous breakdown; becomes interested in literature and reads popular contemporary novels. Loves popular art and illustrations.

1914   Enters middle school in Osaka. Subscribes to haiku magazine *Hototogisu*.

1915   Quits middle school due to parent's financial difficulties. Enters Military Academy in Osaka.

1918   Promoted to Tokyo Central Military Academy.

1919   Dispatched to Army Engineering Battalion 19 in Korea as officer candidate. Reads books on socialism in secret, studies French. Excels with swords and guns.

1920   Enters Army Officers' School. Secretly reads Marx in translation in the local library on holidays. Also reads the Bible in secret. His notebook now exceeds 1,000 haiku.

1921   Quits Army Officers' School. Studies Spanish hoping to emigrate, but gives it up due to family opposition. Reads popular lyric poets, traditional and modern, with enthusiasm. Also reads a study of Tolstoy.

1922   Enters Third School of Higher Education (now Kyoto University), majors in literature. Reads widely, including Nietzsche, Turgenev, and lyrical poets such as Hagiwara Sakutarō, Murō Saisei, and Satō Haruo. Maruyama Kaoru, with whom Miyoshi later coedits *Shiki* (Four seasons), is his classmate.

1925   Graduates from Third School of Higher Education. Enters Tokyo Imperial University majoring in French literature. Fellow students later become leading literary critics, writers, poets. Meets lyrical poet Hori Tatsuo who later invites Miyoshi to coedit *Shiki*.

1926–1927   Writes poetry, joins coterie poetry magazines *Aozora* (Blue sky), *Shii no ki* (Beech tree), *A* (Asia). Receives high commendations on his poetry from readers.

1928   Graduates with major in French literature, joins Ars Press, but as Ars Press folds shortly, makes living as writer. Becomes member of poetry magazine *Shi to shiron* (Poetry and poetics), which publishes his essays on and translations of French poetry.

1930   Devotes himself to translating *Souvenirs entomologiques* by Jean Henri Fabre. First book of poems *Sokuryōsen* (Surveyor ship) published by Daiichishobō is very well received.

1932   *Nansōshū* (Poems from the south window) is published by Shiinokisha.

1934   Publishes his first collection of *tanka*, *Himawari* (Sun flowers) from Shiinokisha, also book of poems *Kankashū* (Poems in the Quiet) from Shikisha. Joins Maruyama Kaoru and Hori Tatsuo to restart poetry magazine *Shiki* (Four seasons).

1935   Translates Baudelaire's *Les fleurs du mal (Flowers of Evil). Sankashū* (Mountain fruits) is published by Shikisha.

1937   Goes to Shanghai on assignment as special literary reporter for magazines *Bungei* (Literature) and *Kaizō* (Reform) upon outbreak of Japan-China Incident. Assigned to file series of reports from battleground.

1939   Collection of books of poems *Haru no misaki* (Headland in spring) is published by Sōgensha; and *Kusasenri* (Grassy crater basin) by Shikisha. Receives an award from Shiika Konwakai (Discussion Group on Traditional and Modern Poetry).

1941   Book of poems *Ittenshō* (Striking one o'clock) is published by Sōgensha.

1942   Plans *Collected Works of Hagiwara Sakutarō* upon Hagiwara's death. Combines his own work in modern and traditional poetry with some essays and publishes as collection titled *Kiryo totose* (A decade of journey) through Usuishobō. Collects "incidental poems on current affairs" containing poems in praise of victory in war, in *Shōhō itaru* (Victorious news arrives), from Stylesha.

1943   *Asanashū* (Morning meals) is published by Seijisha and book of patriotic poems *Kantaku* (Wooden clappers in the cold) is published by Osaka Sōgensha.

1944   *Hanakatami* (Flower basket) is published by Seijisha. Self-publishes *Haru no Tabibito* (Spring traveler). War intensifies. Terminates *Shiki* with its eighty-first issue.

1946   Literary magazine *Shinchō* starts publishing Miyoshi's series of essays titled "Fond Memories of Japan," but halts it as he comes to question Emperor's moral responsibility for war, suggesting his abdication. Publishes books of poetry *Kokyō no hana* (Flowers from home) through Sōgensha and *Suna no toride* (Fort of sand) from Usuishobō.

1951   *Miyoshi Tatsuji senshishū* (Selected poems of Miyoshi Tatsuji) edited by Kawamori Yoshizō, is published by Shinchōsha.

1952   Book of poems, *Rakuda no kobu ni matagatte* (Straddling the camel's hump), and collection of essays on poetics *Takujō no hana* (Flowers on the table) are published by Sōgensha. *Tōshisen* (Selected poems of T'ang Dynasty), coauthored with Yoshikawa Kōjirō, is published by Iwanami shoten.

1953   Receives Geijutsuin shō (Academy of Arts Award) for poetic achievements.

1962   *Teihon Miyoshi Tatsuji zen shi shū* (Authorized complete poems of Miyoshi Tatsuji) is published by Chikumashobō. Becomes member of Academy of Arts.

1963   Awarded Yomiuri Literary Prize for *Teihon Miyoshi Tatsuji zenshishū* (Authorized complete poems of Miyoshi Tatsuji).

1964   Dies of angina in April while engaged in editing *Murō Saisei zenshū* (Complete works of Murō Saisei) with Nakano Shigeharu, Itō Shinkichi, and others.

1964–1966   Chikumashobō publishes twelve-volume collection of Miyoshi's works over two years.

2000   Leading poetry magazine *Gendaishi techō* (Modern Japanese poetry notes) publishes Miyoshi Tatsuji centennial special issue, "Miyoshi Tatsuji: New Discovery."

NAGASE KIYOKO

1906   Born in Okayama Prefecture, family moves to Kanazawa City in Ishikawa Prefecture two years later.

1909   Enters a private kindergarten.

1912   Enrolled in a primary school affiliated with Ishikawa Prefecture Teacher's College.

1922   Graduates from Ishikawa Prefectural Women's School of Higher Education II and enters Hokuriku Women's College. Also takes course on *Man'yō shū* at The Fourth National School of Higher Education in Kanazawa (now Kanazawa University). Moves to Nagoya, Aichi Prefecture, upon father's transfer there.

1924   Reads *Poems of Ueda Bin* and aspires to be poet. Enters Aichi Prefectural Women's School of Higher Education, majoring in English. Gets special instruction in poetry from teachers. Sends her poems to Satō Sōnosuke, brilliant young poet of the time, who offers practical instructions on writing poetry. Becomes member of Satō's new coterie magazine *Shi no ie* (House of poetry).

1927   Marries Nagafune Etsuo, who works for Meiji Insurance Company and lives in Osaka.

1928   First daughter born. *House of Poetry* grows to thirty-member coterie magazine.

1930   Two poems are included in *Nihon josei shi shū* (Poems of Japanese women poets) edited by Inoue Yoshiko. Book of poems, *Guren-*

del no hahaoya (Grendel's mother), is published by Kajinbō, with her mentor Satō's postscript.

1931   Moves to Tokyo upon her husband's transfer. Joins coterie group *Jikan* (Time).

1933   First son is born.

1937   Second daughter is born. Nagafune (husband) drafted into military during Sino-Japanese war and is dispatched to China, where illness keeps him out of fierce battle in which everyone else in his unit is killed. He returns home for long convalescence under medical treatment. Nagase joins newly founded Association of Modern Poets and Association of Women Poets. Contributes eight poems to *Gendai joryū shijin shū* (Poems of modern women poets) published by Yamagashobō.

1940   Book of poems, *Shokoku no ten'nyo* (Heavenly maidens on earth), is published by Kawade Shobō Shinsha.

1943   Complies with request to contribute poem to *Tsuji shi shū* (Tsuji poetry collection) edited by Bungaku Hōkokukai (Literary Association in Support of the Nation), but is displeased with editorial rewrite and printing errors.

1945   As air raids intensify over Tokyo, moves family to live with her mother when Nagafune is transferred to Okayama City and called to military service again. In June most of Okayama City, including children's schools, burns down in air raids. Her family moves to her birthplace, Kumayama, in autumn.

1946   Decides to farm three-quarters of an acre of rice paddies. Nagafune returns from the war. First issue of *Bungaku sai* (Festival of literature) and first coterie poetry magazine published after the war, of which Nagase is a member, appears in January. It sells very well but entire proceeds are embezzled.

1947   Book of poems, *Ōinaru jumoku* (Great big tree), is published by Sakurai shoten. Becomes member of *Shisaku* (Poetry composition).

1948   Book of postwar poems, *Utsukusii kuni* (The beautiful country), is published by Irorishobō. Mother dies.

1949   First recipient of Okayama Cultural Award.

1950   Book of poems, *Honoo ni tsuite* (On flames), is published by Chiyodashoin. Association of Modern Japanese Poets is established; she becomes member.

1951   Nagafune is transferred to Tokyo, but Nagase decides to stay in Okayama with children. Nagase visits Tokyo.

1952   Founds coterie poetry magazine, *Ki bara* (Yellow roses), with six women poets. Farms during daytime, writes only at night. Oldest son enters Waseda University, lives with his father.

1953   Excavation of Tsukinowa ancient burial mound starts. To commemorate its success, writes lyric for *bon* dance, which becomes an annual event.

1954   Book of poems, *Sanjō no shisha* (The dead on the mountaintop), is published by Nihonmiraisha. Includes several poems about incident involving Japanese fishing boat and U.S. nuclear test.

1955   Attends Conference of Asian Countries in New Delhi, representing Women's Association of Kumayama (her local township). Extends trip to China, participates in May Day events. Trip reflects her deep interest in women's issues, social equality issues, peace movement, and antinuclear movement. Returns to plant rice. Supplements income by writing essays and a dozen school songs. Nagafune reaches mandatory retirement age, leaves work at the insurance company, and takes up farming.

1958   Helps to publish newspaper for women.

1963   Becomes acting director, Secretariat of Okayama Council of World Federation of Nations, housed at prefectural office.

1969   *Nagase Kiyoko shishū* (Nagase Kiyoko: selected poems), is published by Shōrinsha.

1972   Book of poems, *Umi wa riku e to* (Sea moving toward land), is published by Shichōsha.

1974   *Tanshō shū* (Aphorisms) is published by Shichōsha.

1977   Books of aphorisms, *Chō no meitei* (Intoxicated butterfly) and *Nagareru kami* (Flowing hair) are published by Shichōsha. Leaves World Federation secretariat and becomes free to write.

1979   Book of poems, *Nagase Kiyoko shishū* (Poems of Nagase Kiyoko), is published by Shichōsha.

1980   Awarded San'yō Newspaper Cultural Prize. *Honoo ni maki o* (Firewood to fire), a book of aphorisms, is published by Shichōsha.

1982   Becomes Chairperson of Okayama Prefecture Poets Association. Japan Modern Poets' Association recognizes her as pioneer in modern Japanese poetry. *Zoku Nagase Kiyoko shi shū* (Poems of Nagase Kiyoko II) is published by Shichōsha.

1983   Book of poems, *Watashi wa chikyū* (I am the earth), is published by Chūsekisha. Founding member and chair of Study Group on Women's History in Okayama.

1984   Book of aphorisms, *Irodori no kumo* (Hues of clouds), is published by Shichōsha. Husband dies.

1987   Awarded Earth Prize for *Akegata ni kuru hito yo* (To you who come at dawn), published by Shichōsha. Women's coterie magazine *Yellow Roses* celebrates thirty-five years of publication.

1988   Holds exhibit of her paintings and poetry in a gallery in Okayama. *Akegata ni kuru hito yo* (To you who come at dawn) receives *Mrs.* Modern Women Poetry Award.

1990   Book of poems, *Himiko yo himiko* (Himiko oh Himiko), is published by Techōsha. *Nagase Kiyoko shishū* (Nagase Kiyoko: selected poems) is published by Shichōsha.

1995   Dies on her birthday February 17, 1995. Twelfth book of new poems, *Haruni nareba uguisu to onajini* (Like a bush warbler when spring comes), is published by Shichōsha in April.

❖

SOURCES

MURŌ SAISEI 室生犀星

The Japanese text and translation are based on *Murō Saisei zenshishū* 室生犀星全詩集 (Complete poems of Murō Saisei) (Tokyo: Chikuma shobō, 1962), compiled and revised by the poet. Poems marked with asterisks are taken from *Murō Saisei, Nihon shijin zenshū* 15 日本詩人全集 15 (Murō Saisei: Complete collection of Japanese poets, vol. 15) (Tokyo: Shinchōsha, 1967), which prints poems as originally published.

Poems are listed in order of appearance in this book.

Ai no shi shū 愛の詩集 (Poems of love) (Tokyo: Kanjō shisha 感情詩社, 1918).

Spring	はる
Morning Song	朝の歌
Winter in My Hometown	故郷にて冬を送る
A Portrait of Dostoyevsky	ドストエフスキイの肖像

Jojō shōkyoku shū 抒情小曲集 (Lyrical songs) (Tokyo: Kanjō shisha 感情詩社, 1918).

Prelude	序曲*
The River Sai	犀川*
Lonely Spring	寂しき春
On a Sand Dune	砂丘の上

Dai ni ai no shi shū 第二愛の詩集 (Poems of love II) (Tokyo: Bunbudō shoten 文武堂書店, 1919).

A Small Home	小さい家庭
After a Concert	音楽会の後*
All in Repose	みな休息して
Aiming at the first light of Dawn	曙光を目ざして

Sabishiki tokai 寂しき都会 (Lonely city) (Tokyo: Shūeikaku 聚英閣, 1920).

Aflame	燃える

Bōshun shi shū 忘春詩集 (Poems of lost spring) (Tokyo: Kyōbunsha 京文社, 1922).

In the Dead of Night	夜半
The Socks	靴下
The Flower of My Family	我が家の花

Aoki uwo o tsuru hito 青き魚を釣る人 (Man fishing blue fish) (Tokyo: Ars アルス, 1923).

The Temple in Spring	春の寺
Mountains	山なみ*
Before the Snow	雪くる前

Tsuru 鶴 (Cranes) (Tokyo: Sojinsha 素人社, 1928)

What I See Inside Myself	己の中に見ゆ

Tori suzume shū 鳥雀集 (Birds and sparrows) (Tokyo: Daiichishobō 第一書房, 1930).

A Valley at Surugadai	駿河台の谷間

Inishi'e いにしへ (Times past) (Tokyo: Ichijōshobō 一条書房, 1943).

The Temple	み寺

| I Will Leave | 帰去来 |
| Look at This Man | この人をみよ |

Yūbae baika 夕映梅花 (Plum blossoms in evening glow) (Tokyo: 1946; included in *Complete poems of Murō Saisei*, 1962).

| Flowers | 花 |

Tabibito 旅びと (Travelers) (Tokyo: Usui shobō 臼井書房, 1947).

| The Sardine | 鰯* |

Ainureba 逢ひぬれば (Encounters) (Tokyo: Fugakuhonsha 富岳本社, 1947).

| Three Years in the Mountains | 三年山中* |

Kinō irasshitte kudasai 昨日いらっしってください (Please come back yesterday) (Tokyo: Satsuki shobō 五月書房, 1959).

| Please Come Back Yesterday | 昨日いらっしってください |

Ban'nen 晩年 (Late years) in *Murō Saisei: Nihon shijin zenshū 15* (Murō Saisei: Complete collection of Japanese poets, vol. 15).

| To Someone | 誰かに |
| Song of an Old Prawn | 老いたるえびのうた* |

❖

KANEKO MITSUHARU　金子光晴

The Japanese text and translation are based on *Teihon Kaneko Mitsuharu zenshishu* 定本金子光晴全詩集 (Authorized complete poems of Kaneko Mitsuharu) (Tokyo: Chikuma shobō 筑摩書房, 1967).

Poems are listed in order of appearance in this book.

Koganemushi 金亀子 (*Gold beetle*) (Tokyo: Shinchōsha 新潮社, 1923).

    Gold Beetle　　　　　　　　　　　金亀子

Mizu no rurō 水の流浪 (Vagrant water) (Tokyo: Shinchōsha 新潮社, 1926).

    Short Pieces on the Sea　　　　　海の小品
        Seagulls　　　　　　　　　　　鷗
        At the Lighthouse　　　　　　燈臺にて
    Used Shoe Shop　　　　　　　　　古靴店
    (On the Reservoir)　　　　　　　　(上水にて) (Left out of *Vagrant Water*, but included in *Zenshishū*)

Fuka shizumu 鱶沈む (Sharks sink) (Tokyo: Ariakesha 有明社, 1927).

    Kanzanji Temple　　　　　　　　寒山寺

Robō no aijin 路傍の愛人 (Lovers on the roadside) (published in Kagaribi 篝火, 1928).

    Night in Pedang　　　　　　　　ペダンの夜

Same 鮫 (Sharks) (Tokyo: Jinminsha 人民社, 1937).

    The Lighthouse　　　　　　　　　燈台

On'na tachi e no eregii 女たちへのエレジー (An elegy for women) (Tokyo: Sōgensha 創元社, 1949).

    Washbasin　　　　　　　　　　　洗面器

Rakkasan 落下傘 (Parachute) (Tokyo: Nihon miraiha hakkōsho 日本未来派発行所, 1948).

Song of Dawn: A Prefatory Poem	あけがたの歌
Angels	天使

Oni no ko no uta 鬼の児の歌 (Songs of the ogre's children) (Tokyo: Jūjiya shoten 十字屋書店, 1949).

A Song of the Egg	卵の唄
Ogres and Poet	鬼と詩人
Ascension	昇天

Ga 蛾 (*Moths*) (Tokyo: Hokutoshoin 北斗書院, 1948).

Moths II	蛾 II
Moths III	蛾 III
Sphere	球
Rain	雨
Mount Fuji	富士
(Snow)	(雪) (Left out of *Moths*, but included in *Zenshishū*)
(Fog)	(霧) (Left out of *Moths*, but included in *Zenshishū*)

Ningen no higeki 人間の悲劇 (Tragedy of man) (Tokyo: Sōgensha 創元社, 1952.)

— On Autobiography	— 自叙伝について

Hijō 非情 (Heartless) (Tokyo: Shinchōsha 新潮社, 1955)

Heart	心
Reeds	葦

❖

MIYOSHI TATSUJI 三好達治

The Japanese text and translation are based on *Teihon Miyoshi Tatsuji zenshishū* (Authorized complete poems of Miyoshi Tatsuji) 定本三好達治全詩集, (Tokyo: Chikumashobō 筑摩書房, 1964).

Poems are listed in order of appearance in this book.

Sokuryōsen 測量船 (*Surveyor Ship*) (Tokyo: Daiichishobō 第一書房, 1930).

The Youth*	少年
The Lake	湖水
A Village*	村
Crow	鴉

Nansō shū 南窻集 (Poems from the South Window) (Tokyo: Shii no ki sha 椎の木社, 1932).

Signal*	信号
Earth*	土

Sanka shū 山果集 (Mountain fruits) (Tokyo: Shikisha 四季社, 1935).

Lamb*	仔羊
Scenery on a Plate	皿の中の風景
Turtledove	山鳩

Tsuchifuru 霾 (Dust devil) (in *Haru no misaki* 春の岬) (Tokyo: Sōgensha 創元社, 1939)

Self Portrait	自画像

Kusasenri 艸千里 (Grassy crater basin) (Tokyo: Shikisha 四季社, 1939).

Tears	涙
Hail Comes Fluttering 2*	あられふりける二
Paulownia Flowers	桐の花

Ittenshō 一点鐘 (Striking one o'clock) (Tokyo: Sōgensha 創元社, 1941).

    Family*　　　　　　　　　　　家庭
    Broken Window　　　　　　　　毀れた窓
    Mysterious Music　　　　　　　　謎の音楽

Kantaku 寒柝 (Wooden clappers in the cold) (Osaka: Osaka Sōgensha 大阪創元社, 1943).

    May the *Koto*'s　　　　　　　　ことのねたつな
      Resonance Soar*

Hanagatami 花筐 (Flower basket) (Tokyo: Seijisha 青磁社, 1944).

    Call My Name*　　　　　　　　わが名をよびて

Left out of *Kokyō no hana* 故郷の花 (Flowers from home) (Tokyo: Sōgensha 創元社, 1946)

    After We were Defeated　　　　我ら戦争に敗れたあとに
      at War

Suna no toride 砂の砦 (Fort of sand) (Tokyo: Usuishobō 臼井書房, 1946).

    In Praise of the Walnut*　　　　　胡桃讃

Rakuda no kobu ni matagatte 駱駝の瘤にまたがって (Straddling the camel's hump) (Tokyo: Sōgensha 創元社, 1952).

    Verses on a Village Brew*　　　　村酒雑詠
    This Slope Brings Back Memories　なつかしい斜面
    Yet, a Stirring in Me Seems*　　　けれども情緒は

Hyakutabi no nochi 百たびののち (After one hundred times), collected in *zenshishū*, 1962.

    The Shore of the Sky*　　　　　　空のなぎさ

*Earlier versions of translations marked with asterisks appeared in 2010 at https://www.poetryinternationalweb.net/pi/site/country/item/31/Japan

❖

NAGASE KIYOKO　永瀬清子

The Japanese text and translation are based on the following sources, organized by initial publication dates of the original poems.

Nagase Kiyoko shishū 永瀬清子詩集 (Poems of Nagase Kiyoko) (Tokyo: Shichōsha 思潮社, 1979).
Zoku Nagase Kiyoko shishū 続永瀬清子詩集 *(Poems of Nagase Kiyoko II*) (Tokyo: Shichōsha 思潮社, 1982).
Nagase Kiyoko shishū 永瀬清子詩集 (Selected poems of Nagase Kiyoko) (Tokyo: Shichōsha 思潮社, 1990).
Damashite kudasai kokoro yasashiku だましてください言葉やさしく (Humor me with your sweet words) (Tokyo: Dōwaya 童話屋 2008).
Poems are listed in order of appearance in this book.

Grendel no hahaoya グレンデルの母親 (Grendel's mother) (Tokyo: Kajinbo 歌人房, 1930).

Grendel's Mother	グレンデルの母親は

Shokoku no ten'nyo 諸国の天女 (Heavenly maidens on earth) (Tokyo: Kawade shobōshinsha 河出書房新社, 1940).

Heavenly Maidens* 　on Earth	諸国の天女

Ōinaru jumoku 大いなる樹木 (A great big tree) (Tokyo: Sakurai shoten 桜井書店, 1947).

A Great Big Tree*	大いなる樹木
Early Spring	早春
On a Day with a Gentle Breeze*	そよ風のふく日に

Utsukushii kuni 美しい国 (Beautiful country) (Tokyo: Irorishobō 爐書房, 1948).

The Ring of Dancers	踊りの輪
Burning a Light at Night*	夜に燈ともし
Beautiful Country	美しい国

Honoo ni tsuite 焔について (On flames) (Tokyo: Chiyodashoin 千代田書院, 1950).

Humor Me with Your Sweet Words*	だましてください 言葉やさしく
Song of a Woman*	女のうたえる
You in the Shade of a Tree*	木陰の人
Why Like This	なぜこんなに
Flames	焔について

Bara shi shū 薔薇詩集 (Poems of roses) (Tokyo: Matobashobō 的場書房, 1958).

Vortex	渦
The Fleeting Moment*	束の間
Seedlings	苗
Dawn*	夜あけ

Sanjō no shisha 山上の死者 (The dead on the mountaintop) (Tokyo: Nihon miraiha 日本未来派, 1954).

To Fit My Feet*	私の足に
Snake	蛇

Umi wa riku e to 海は陸へと (The sea toward the land) (Tokyo: Shichōsha 思潮社, 1972).

I am the Earth*	私は地球
The Third Eye	第三の目
Thinking It Was Coal	石炭と思って

Zoku Nagase Kiyoko shi shū 続永瀬清子詩集 (Poems of Nagase Kiyoko II) (Tokyo: Shichōsha 思潮社, 1982).

My Rival Was "Death"*	ライバルは「死」であった

Akegata ni kuru hito yo あけがたにくる人よ (To you who come at dawn) (Tokyo: Shichōsha 思潮社, 1987).

  To You Who Come   あけがたにくる人よ
    at Dawn
  My Aged Demon   老いたるわが鬼女

Damashite kudasai kotoba yasashiku だましてください言葉やさしく (Humor me with your sweet words) (Tokyo: Dōwaya 童話屋, 2008).

  My Dear Silent One,   黙っている人よ
    My Indigo Mist*   藍色の靄よ

Tanshō shu 短章集 (Aphorisms) (Tokyo: Shichōsha 思潮社, 2007)

  When a Truck Comes and   トラックが来て私を轢
    Runs Over Me*   いたとき
  What Is a Poet?*   詩人とは何か
  Why I Write Poetry*   詩を書く理由
  Poetry Is*   詩は
  Poetry Needs Rhythm*   詩にリズムが

❖

*Earlier versions of translations marked with asterisks appeared in 2009 at https://www.poetryinternationalweb.net/pi/site/country/item/31/Japan

BIBLIOGRAPHY

Andō, Motoo, Ōoka Makoto, Nakamura Minoru, eds. *Gendaishi daijiten* [Encyclopedia of modern Japanese poetry]. Tokyo: Sanseidō, 2008.
Andō, Tsuguo. *Gendaishi no tenkai* [Evolution of modern Japanese poetry]. Tokyo: Shichōsha, 1969.
Ayukawa, Nobuo. *Ayukawa Nobuo shironshū* [Collected critical essays on poetry by Ayukawa Nobuo]. Tokyo: Shichōsha, 1970.
Ikubo, Itoko. *Josei shi no naka no Nagase Kiyoko—sengo hen* [Nagase Kiyoko in the course of women's history: postwar period]. Tokyo: Domesushuppan, 2009.
Itō, Sei, Yoshida Seiichi, Bundō Junsaku, Koumi Eiji, eds. *Gendaishi no kanshō 1–4* [Appreciating modern Japanese poetry vol. 1–4]. Tokyo: Meijishoin, 1968.
Itō, Shinkichi. *Shi no furusato* [Birthplaces of poems]. Tokyo: Shinchōsha, 1974.
Jansen, Marius B. *The Making of Modern Japan*. Cambridge, MA: Harvard University Press, 2000.
Japan, an Illustrated Encyclopedia I & II. New York: Kodansha America, 1993
Japanese National Commission for Unesco, comp. *Japan, Its Land, People and Culture*. Tokyo: Ministry of Finance, 1964.
Kaneko, Mitsuharu. *Teihon Kaneko Mitsuharu zenshishū* [Authorized complete poems of Kaneko Mitsuharu]. Tokyo: Chikuma shobō, 1967.
Kaneko, Mitsuharu/Kusano, Shinpei. *Nihon shijin zenshū 24* [Kaneko Mitsuharu / Kusano Shinpei, Complete collection of Japanese poets 24]. Tokyo: Shinchōsha, 1967.

Kaneko, Mitsuharu. *Shijin: Kaneko Mitshuaru jiden* [Poet: Autobiography of Kaneko Mitsuharu]. Tokyo: Kōdansha, 1994.
Kawamori, Yoshizō, ed. *Miyoshi Tatsuji shishū* [Selected poems of Miyoshi Tatsuji]. Tokyo: Shinchōsha, 1951.
Keene, Donald. *Emperor of Japan–Meiji and His World 1852–1912*. New York: Columbia University Press, 2002.
Kihara, Kōichi. "*Sengo shi monogatari*" [Tale of the postwar poetry]. *Eureka: shi to hihyō* vols. 2–13. (Eureka: poetry and criticism). Tokyo: Seidosha, 1970.
Kumayama-cho Nagase Kiyoko no satozukuri suishin iinkai, ed. *Shijin Nagase Kiyoko sakuhinshū* [Works of a poet Nagase Kiyoko]. Okayama: Kumayama-cho, 1996.
Merwin, W.S. *Selected Translations 1948–2011*. Port Townsend, WA: Copper Canyon Press, 2013.
Miyoshi, Tatsuji. *Haru no misaki* [Headland in spring]. Tokyo: Sōgensha, 1945.
―――. *Teihon Miyoshi Tatsuji zenshishū* [Authorized complete poems of Miyoshi Tatsuji]. Tokyo: Chikumashobō, 1962.
―――. *Miyoshi Tatsuji, Nihon shijin zenshū 21* [Miyoshi Tatsuji: Complete collection of Japanese poets vol. 21]. Tokyo: Shinchōsha, 1967.
―――. *Miyoshi Tatsuji*. Gendaishi bunko 1038. Tokyo: Shichōsha, 1989.
Murō, Saisei. *Murō Saisei, Nihon shijin zenshū 15* [Murō Saisei: Complete collection of Japanese poets vol. 15]. Tokyo: Shinchōsha, 1971.
―――. *Murō Saisei zenshishū* [Complete poems of Murō Saisei]. Tokyo: Chikumashobō, 1962.
Nakano, Shigeharu, ed. *Murō Saisei shishū* [Selected poems of Murō Saisei]. Tokyo: Shinchōsha, 1951.
Nagase, Kiyoko. *Nagase Kiyoko shishū* [Poems of Nagase Kiyoko]. Tokyo: Shichōsha, 1979.
―――. *Zoku Nagase Kiyoko shishū* [Poems of Nagase Kiyoko II]. Tokyo: Shichōsha, 1982.
―――. *Nagase Kiyoko*. Gendaishi bunko 1039. Tokyo: Shichōsha, 1990.
―――. *Tanshō shū* [Aphorisms]. Tokyo: Shichōsha, 2007.
―――. *Tanshō shū zoku* [Aphorisms II]. Tokyo: Shichōsha, 2008.

———. *Damashite kudasai kotoba yasashiku* [Humor me with your gentle words]. Tokyo: Dowaya, 2008.

Ōoka, Makoto. *Tōji no kakei: nihon gendaishi no ayumi* [A prodigal son's descendants: Evolution of modern Japanese poetry]. Tokyo: Shichōsha, 1969.

———. *The Colors of Poetry, Essays on Classic Japanese Verse*. Translated by Takako and Thomas Lento. Michigan: Katydid Books, Oakland University, 1991.

———. *Shōwa shishi* [History of Shōwa Poetry]. Tokyo: Shichōsha, 1977.

———. *Gendai no shijintachi 1&2* [Modern Japanese poets 1&2]. Tokyo: Seidosha, 1981.

Tanikawa, Shuntarō, ed. *Miyoshi Tatsuji shishū* [Selected poems of Miyoshi Tatsuji]. Tokyo: Yayoishobō, 1965.

Yoshida, Ken'ichi. *Shi ni tsuite* [On poetry]. Tokyo: Eurika, 1975.

TITLES IN THE NEW JAPANESE HORIZON SERIES

The Art of Being Alone: Tanikawa Shuntarō Poems 1952–2009
translated with introduction by Takako U. Lento (2011)

Indian Summer by Kanai Mieko
translated with introduction by Tomoko Aoyama and Barbara Hartley (2012)

Of Birds Crying by Minako Ōba
translated with introduction by Michiko N. Wilson and Michael K. Wilson (2011)

Pioneers of Modern Japanese Poetry: Murō Saisei, Kaneko Mitsuharu, Miyoshi Tatsuji, Nagase Kiyoko
translated with introduction by Takako Lento (2019)

Red Ghost, White Ghost: Stories and Essays by Kita Morio
translated with introduction by Masako Inamoto (2018)

Running Boy by Megumu Sagisawa
translated with introduction by Tyran Grillo (2019)

Single Sickness and Other Stories by Misuda Mizuko
translated with introduction by Lynne Kutsukake (2011)

The Wasteland (Arano) by Takako Takahashi
translated with introduction by Britten Dean (2019)

eap.einaudi.cornell.edu/publications

www.ingramcontent.com/pod-product-compliance
Lightning Source LLC
Chambersburg PA
CBHW031702230426
43668CB00006B/82